CHARLIE WHISTLER'S OMNIUM GATHERUM

CHARLIE WHISTLER'S OMNIUM GATHERUM

Campfire Stories and Adirondack Adventures

PHILIP DELVES BROUGHTON

WITH ILLUSTRATIONS BY

Robert Parker

Sarah Nicholls

Nancy Loeber

HARPER

An Imprint of HarperCollins*Publishers*

For AUGIE *and* HUGO

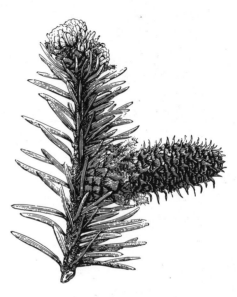

Energy is eternal delight.

—WILLIAM BLAKE

CHARLES W. WHISTLERS & THEIR OMNIUM GATHERUMS

Charles Wilberforce Whistler, b. 1840, Vol. I

Charles Wetherby Whistler, b. 1860, Vol. II

Charles Watson Whistler, b. 1891, Vol. III

Charles Wilfred Whistler, b. 1935, Vol. IV

Charles Warren Whistler, b. 1970, Vol. V

Charles Welsh Whistler, b. 2002, Vol. VI

This evening

HI,

My name is Charlie Whistler. And what you are holding in your hands is my "Omnium Gatherum." Well, I say "my," but really it's ours, meaning my family's. And now that you're reading it, it's yours too. So let's just call it *an* Omnium Gatherum.

I'm writing to you sitting on the dock at our cabin on Raquette Lake in the Adirondacks, a land of lakes, mountains, and forests about five hours north of New York City. In the summer, it's cool and green. In the winter it fills with snow. You could live several lifetimes and never see it all.

The cabin is right on the water. It was built more than a hundred years ago by my great-great-great-grandfather Charlie. The floors are splintery. The bedsheets are worn and thin. The plumbing often breaks down. But for generations of Whistlers, it's been our favorite place in the world. We come and go from June to September, when it's warm and the blackfly isn't about. We come at weekends when Mom's and Dad's work allows, and for a couple of weeks every August. But a few hardy Whistlers have seen out entire years up here, sitting through the long deep winters in flannel pajamas beside a well-fed stove.

Right now, the sun is setting. We've eaten supper. Mom and Dad are reading and my kid sister Ella is taking her bath. We went canoeing out to the far side of the lake today and she started yelling because she saw a loon, her favorite bird.

Loons, aka "hell divers," have this trick where they'll be drifting along beside you on the water, then suddenly they'll disappear and pop up a hundred

yards away cackling this witchy cackle as if they've put one over on you. Ella thinks this is the greatest. She doesn't care that on shore they're the clumsiest-looking beasts you ever saw or that their cry sounds like they're inviting you to a funeral. When I call her a loon, she takes it as a compliment. She's contrary like that. This afternoon, she was pointing and screaming at one of these crafty loons and in her excitement, she capsized her boat. One minute you couldn't hear yourself think for all the noise she was making. Then silence. A gurgling sound. I paddled hard over to where she had gone under, searching for signs of her. Then like one of her favorite loons, she popped up a way away with a whole lot of splashing and more screaming. "Charlie! Save me!" She loves to be dramatic. It took us half an hour of yanking and twisting to drag her boat to the shore, empty it, and get her back in it.

Anyway, now that she's upstairs, I have a few minutes of peace and I've been meaning to write this for a while. You see, it turns out I come from a family of writers. Not the kind who write books or movies. But letter writers, scribblers, doodlers, the kind who leave long notes on the refrigerator, because often they'd rather write than talk.

I found this out last year, after my Grandpa died. He was a great man. Kind and patient even with a yappy kid like me. Things I'd do that would drive my parents crazy would just make him laugh. Break a plate? Laugh. Jump naked into the lake? Laugh. Sneak an extra pancake? Laugh. Deflate another kid's bike tires? Laugh. Shampoo the dog and style his hair into a Mohawk? Laugh. But, as I said, he died and left this house to my Dad.

Before Grandpa died, he promised me I could have his old snowshoes. I'd been pestering Dad for a while about finding them, and one day he put down his coffee and newspaper and took me up to the attic. It was a mess up there, racks of threadbare suits and shirts, bags full of shoes, and a few old trunks crammed to bursting. I thought it would only take a few minutes to find what I was looking for. But Dad and I ended up spending hours. There were old toys and stacks of curling photographs showing Whistlers past and present during their summers on the lake. Dad found an old chair and leafed through them slowly, each one prompting a memory or story.

And then under a stack of clothes, I found an old leather folder held together with elastic bands. On the cover were the words "Omnium Gatherum."

Inside was a jumble of papers, some handwritten, some typed. There were letters and newspaper clippings and short scribbles. Many were illustrated with drawings and maps, or had photographs stapled to them. I sat down on the floor to read. Some of the pages were so old, their edges crumbled between my fingers.

The earliest letters came from the late 1870s. And many were addressed to or written by "Charlie." It's not just my name. It's my Dad's name, my grandfather's name, and his father's name, going back many generations. We're all Charlie Whistler.

The letters were from members of our family, cousins, uncles, aunts, brothers, sisters, parents. They told the most amazing stories, of danger in distant lands, of risk-taking closer to home. There were stories about cowboys and adventurers and advice on everything from cooking to scaring off grizzly bears. There were pictures and paintings and poems.

When I showed them to Dad, he held them for a moment and then beckoned me downstairs. He went to a drawer in his study and pulled out another file, like the one I'd found. "I'd been meaning to show these to you," he said. This was his own Omnium Gatherum, bulging with postcards he'd received, drawings he'd made as a kid, clippings from newspapers and magazines. "'Omnium Gatherum' is fake Latin for a place where you collect all kinds of random things. Could be a kitchen drawer or a scrapbook like this. Your grandfather used to say that the more curious we are about one thing, whether it's sports or nature or science, the more we take pleasure in everything." The stack of papers wobbled on his lap. "Add all this up, it explains who we are. You should make one yourself, Charlie. Use the old ones to get started."

We went back up to the attic and filled a few boxes with the papers we'd found up there. There were a few more Omnium Gatherums buried in all the mess, compiled by Whistlers past. I spread them all out on the living room floor in front of the cold fireplace, drawings in one stack, letters in another, maps in another, and so on. I've had to try to limit the damage when Max our dog decides to come inside after a swim and shake himself dry, spraying water everywhere. I've been going through the stacks slowly all summer—whenever

4

Ella's not pretending to drown—picking out the items I like and adding a few of my own. I like to do it in the early morning before anyone else is up, when it's still cool outside and the mist is still lying across the lake. No one's hassling me to pack my bag for school or pinging me with texts. There's not even a TV up here, so Ella sleeps late. In those quiet hours, I can almost hear these generations of Whistlers talking to me. It's like they're sitting in the cabin, their feet up on a stool, slapping the arm of their chair and howling with laughter one minute, leaning forward and talking in a spooky whisper the next. It's as if it's important to them that I know this stuff, that I see the world the way they did. They want me to be just as curious and adventurous as they were, to live a big life—or as my Dad says when he's feeling grumpy, not a life shrunk to the size of a screen. I don't feel any time separates me from all these Whistlers past. I know exactly who they are. They are part of me.

I've tried to keep everything in chronological order, except when I haven't. You can call that the compiler's privilege. My Omnium Gatherum. My order.

I hope you like it.

When you come to Raquette Lake, we'll talk more.

Your friend,
Charlie

July 1878

I have decided to purchase land and build a house here in the Adirondacks. It may be the grandest folly I've ever undertaken, or a stroke of genius. Either way, I blame two men for my action. The first is that scoundrel Henry David Thoreau. Until recently, my life had been moving along just fine. From home to school to a fine job as a merchant in New York City, I have always been thoroughly respectable and, I thought, content. But Thoreau has bullied me into looking at my life afresh—and sown disorder.

The trouble started one spring evening, when I returned home after another busy day of buying and selling, hung up my coat, grunted at the children, who had lined up in their pajamas to greet me, and marched into my study. Such unforgivable self-importance, I regret to say, had become my natural mode of behavior.

I still had business to attend to. But soon after 10 p.m. when the house was quiet, I settled down with a cigar and noticed that beside my armchair, my wife, Eleanor, had placed a copy of Thoreau's *Walden*. Friends had told me of Thoreau. They suggested he was nothing more than a crank, a work-shy grumbler, that he couldn't cope with ordinary life, so had escaped into the woods near Boston for a couple of years, built himself a cabin, and written up the experience. His book hardly sounded like a page-turner!

But I felt I should find out for myself. I anticipated that by 10:30 I'd be done.

At 1:00 in the morning, I finally set *Walden* down. My cigar had long ago burned out and the fire in the hearth was nothing but ash. "Simplicity, simplicity, simplicity!" Thoreau had urged. His words stung.

How many times had Eleanor found me pacing around my study fretting about business, how to pay for this or that, all the while ignoring my own family? Life was too short to be wasted on worry, she told me. But somehow the message never pierced my thick skull. It had been weeks since I had read the children a bedtime story, months since I had even engaged them in a proper conversation. I saw life as a greasy pole, with my job being to shimmy myself and my family up it. I was doing the opposite of what Thoreau suggested. My life was complexity, complexity, complexity!

Every word he wrote haunted me. "I went to the woods because I wished to live deliberately, to front only the essential facts of life, and see if I could not learn what it had to teach, and not, when I came to die, discover that I had not lived. I wanted to live deep and suck out all the marrow of life, to live so sturdily and Spartan-like as to put to rout all that was not life, to cut a broad swath and shave close, to drive life into a corner, and reduce it to its lowest terms, and, if it proved to be mean, why then to get the whole and genuine meanness of it, and publish its meanness to the world; or if it were sublime, to know it by experience, and be able to give a true account of it in my next excursion." And he had done so. Far too well.

I barely slept that night, and the next day canceled all my meetings. Instead, I arranged to meet my old friend Kermit Looden in the graveyard of Trinity Church, near Wall Street. There, surrounded by the dead, we spoke. Kermit is a bookseller and lives his life at least two steps back from the boiling whitewater of my own. He listened to my ravings about Thoreau and sucking the marrow and Spartan living and concluded, "You need to get some fresh air."

I pointed around us, to the skies above Manhattan. He shook his head.

"Proper fresh air. I am taking you to the Adirondacks."

I knew a little of this vast wilderness far north of New York City. I had read of its lakes and trees and bears. But I had never been. I had camped as a child, of course, but it had been years since I had slept on the ground or eaten out of a tin under moonlight. Kermit handed me a recent copy of *The Atlantic Monthly*, folded open to an article about Old Phelps, an Adirondack guide. "He'll show us around."

The following weekend, we arrived at a small lodge on Saranac Lake. Phelps was sitting on a log, smoking a short pipe, waiting for us. I could try to describe him, but the writer for the *Atlantic* did it for me. "A sturdy figure, with long body and short legs, clad in a woolen shirt and butternut-colored trousers repaired to the point of picturesqueness, his head surmounted by a limp, light brown felt hat, frayed away at the top, so that his yellowish hair grew out of it like some nameless fern out of a pot. His tawny hair was long and tangled, matted now many years past the possibility of being entered by a comb. His features were small and delicate, and set in the frame of a reddish beard, the razor having mowed away a clearing about the sensitive mouth, which was not seldom wreathed with a childlike and charming smile. Out of this hirsute environment looked the small grey eyes, set near together; eyes that made you believe instinct can grow into philosophic judgment. His feet and hands were of aristocratic smallness, although the latter were not worn away by ablutions; in fact, they assisted his toilet to give you the impression that here was a man who had just come out of the ground—a real son of the soil, whose appearance was partially explained by his humorous relation to soap. 'Soap is a thing,' he said, 'that I hain't no kinder use for.' His clothes seemed to have been put on him once and for all, like the bark of a tree, a long time ago."

His voice was shrill and trembling, more like the cry of a bird than a human. Once we were out in the wild, his age seemed to slide right off him. He sauntered along the narrow mountain paths and clambered over rocks with all the energy of a ten-year-old. A "reg'lar walk" for him was along a beaten track. A "random scoot" took us plunging along untrodden paths. Time had no meaning for him. If there was a sunset to be admired, he admired it in full, waiting until the last rays had disappeared. If there was a flower to be smelled, he bent over and breathed it in deeply. At night as we ate, he told us he owned nothing nor felt the need to. The Adirondacks were his home. If someone were to take away the hut where he spent his winters, he trusted these mountains to yield up a spot where he could build another one.

Old Phelps was the freest man I had ever met. He seemed to live on nothing but apples and the smoke from his pipe. I envied him.

Thoreau was fond of a story in the *Gulistan*, one of the great works of Persian literature. It tells of the cypress tree, which was known to Persians as "azad" or free. Other trees may bloom or wither, but the cypress is constant, always flourishing, though never bearing fruit. The lesson of the cypress, a wise man explained, is that only when we have nothing to give away are we truly free.

I'm not prepared to give up my work or my family or my responsibilities in the city. There are certain things I don't want to be free of. But with this house, I am making an effort to be less the fretting bearer of fruit and more like the cypress. And I hope my children will be too, constant, flourishing, and free. This place, this house, I believe will serve as a foundation for the Whistlers to meet the world on their terms and no others. We break ground next week.

If Orson Phelps had lived in Japan, they'd have called him "wabi-sabi." "Wabi" describes someone or something which is perfectly itself, at one with nature, free of greed, dissatisfaction, or anger. The Japanese use the example of a joyful old monk in his wind-torn robe. In the Adirondacks, it's an old guide happily sitting on a log in his worn-out trousers. "Sabi" describes the beautiful effects of time. It is the beauty of an ancient stone step, when you think of all the feet that have worn it down. It is a falling-down tobacco barn, driftwood, or the moss on a garden bench. It is the stem of a wilting flower, or the creased smile in an elderly person's face.

A SHORT HISTORY OF THE ADIRONDACKS

A d-i-ron'dacks means "tree-eaters." It was used by the Iroquois to insult their enemies, the Algonquins. Algonquins were "Ratirontacks," wood eaters, forest Indians, whereas the Iroquois were Ratinonsionni, "those who build cabins," and thought themselves more civilized. Soon after the English took control of New Netherland and renamed it New York, they began chopping down the trees of the Adirondack forests. The loggers grew rich, but the Indians lost their homes. After the Revolutionary War, the State of New York sold yet more land to loggers in order to pay off debts incurred in the war. By the mid-nineteenth century, the situation was dire. The woods were vanishing and the soil was eroding. With less soil to soak up the rainfall, there were many more floods. An unusual man came to the Adirondacks' rescue. Verplanck Colvin was the son of a wealthy lawyer who at the age of 18 decided to devote himself to crisscrossing and mapping the Adirondack wilderness. He was the first to climb several of the region's highest mountains. He created a detailed map of the Adirondacks and persuaded the government of New York State that the destruction of its forests would reduce the water flowing into the surrounding rivers and canals. "Unless the region be preserved essentially in its present wilderness condition," he wrote in 1874, "the ruthless burning and destruction of

11

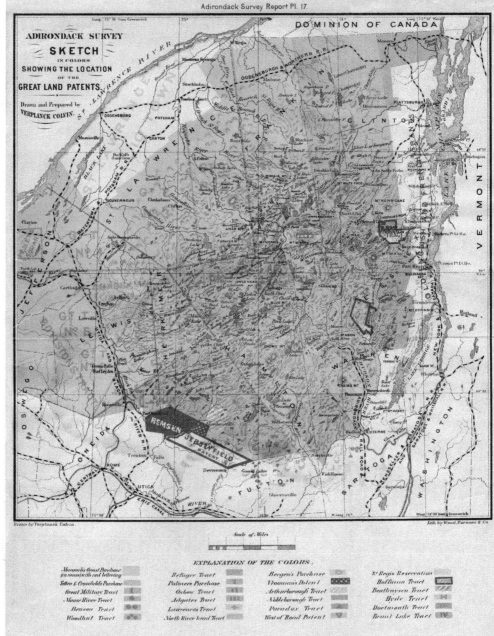

ADIRONDACK SURVEY
SKETCH
IN COLORS
SHOWING THE LOCATION
OF THE
GREAT LAND PATENTS.
Drawn and Prepared by
VERPLANCK COLVIN.

DOMINION OF CANADA

VERMONT

EXPLANATION OF THE COLORS.

Macomb's Great Purchase (in mass) with red lettering
Totten & Crossfield's Purchase
Great Military Tract
Moose River Tract
Benson Tract
Woodhull Tract

Refugee Tract
Palmers Purchase
Oxbow Tract
Adgates Tract
Lawrences Tract
North River head Tract

Bergen's Purchase
Vrooman's Patent
Arthurborough Tract
Nobleborough Tract
Paradox Tract
West of Road Patent

St Regis Reservation
Hoffman Tract
Beaufhuysen Tract
Hyde Tract
Dartmouth Tract
Brant Lake Tract

the forest will slowly, year after year, creep onward . . . and vast areas of naked rock, arid sand and gravel will alone remain to receive the bounty of the clouds, unable to retain it." This led eventually to New York State declaring the Adirondack forests "forever wild." A total of 6.1 million acres of mountains and forests, an area the size of Vermont, would be kept for recreational use—no more logging. All thanks to Verplanck.

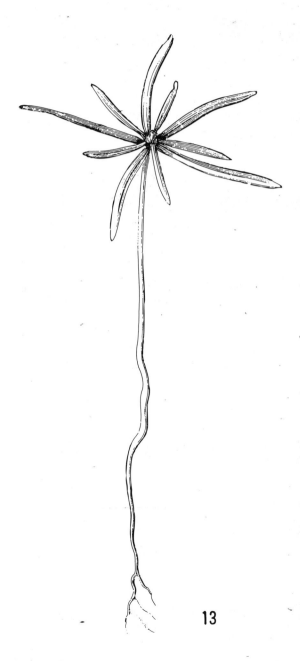

'From OG Vol. I, Summer 1892.

A young Irishman called William Butler Yeats clearly shares the Whistler passion for lakes and cabins! And knows how it feels to be stuck in the city. We should invite him to Raquette and clear room for his nine rows of beans and his hive.

THE LAKE ISLE OF INNISFREE

BY W. B. YEATS

I will arise and go now, and go to Innisfree,
And a small cabin build there, of clay and wattles made;
Nine bean-rows will I have there, a hive for the honey-bee,
And live alone in the bee-loud glade.

And I shall have some peace there, for peace comes dropping slow,
Dropping from the veils of the morning to where the cricket sings;
There midnight's all a glimmer, and noon a purple glow,
And evening full of the linnet's wings.

I will arise and go now, for always night and day
I hear lake water lapping with low sounds by the shore;
While I stand on the roadway, or on the pavements grey,
I hear it in the deep heart's core.

From OG Vol. I, 1884.

Up at the carry by Raquette Falls, staggering along with my canoe braced over my shoulders, I crashed into a man in a straw hat sitting on a rock beside the path. He had dropped his fishing rods and nets at his feet and was sketching feverishly. He didn't hear me and I didn't see him before I rammed him with my boat. Said his name was Winslow Homer and he came to the Adirondacks to fish and paint. After he'd picked up his things and we'd both dusted ourselves off, we fell to talking. From his sketches, I could see he was no gentleman amateur. He wielded his pencil like a master. He had been watching a fly-fisherman casting from a boat out on the lake and trying to convey the motion of his rod in preparation for a painting in oil. The hardest thing about painting a fishing scene, he said, was the moment when the painting was finished except for the fishing line itself. To achieve the kind of sweeping line he wanted, he would finish the whole painting, then take a deep breath and cut through the paint with one great sweep of a razor, as if casting his fly rod—

and hope he didn't cut through the canvas as well. We wished each other well and he said if I ever found myself in Prout's Neck, Maine, I should visit his studio. But how would I find it? He told me to look for a sign on the path that read "Snakes, Snakes, Mice." He had put it there himself to deter the unwanted visitor. But I should ignore it as I was most welcome.

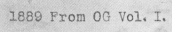

The Fourth of July here on Raquette Lake means flags, food, disorderly games, and fireworks. The one Whistler rule on this day of American days is that you show the spirit of those daring few who threw out the British. Sing, eat, play, and damn the consequences.

We begin on the porch before breakfast with our national anthem. No excuses. Doesn't matter if you're the lead tenor in the Metropolitan Opera or can't sing better than a mule with toothache. You are expected at 7:00 a.m. precisely. Pajamas are accepted. Bad attitudes are not.

There are two things which please me most about our national anthem. First is how hard it is to sing. It goes low, then high, then low again—torture for the ordinary bathtub warbler. If it were easier to sing, we'd flog it to death. Instead, we save it for when we need it.

Second are the question marks. Say, can you see? You see that flag still flying? This isn't some rollicking air, full of self-congratulation and boasting. It's about astonishment and gratitude that this country of ours exists.

The story of our anthem's composition goes that in September 1814, the merchant ships of our young country were jostling with the warring French and British for control of the Atlantic. The British had burned down Washington, D.C. And on their way back to their ships, a group of dragoons stopped at the home of Dr. William Beanes in Upper Marlboro, Maryland. Beanes was hosting a party to celebrate the fact his town hadn't been burned down. The dragoons helped themselves to his punch bowl,

but Beanes ordered them off his property. They grabbed him and marched him off to a British ship to court-martial him for rudeness.

Francis Scott Key, a local lawyer, was sent by President James Madison to try to rescue the kidnapped doctor. Key sailed down the Chesapeake and found the British fleet at anchor at the mouth of the Potomac. He pleaded with the British admiral, George Cockburn, for Beanes's release. Yes, perhaps Beanes should have shared his punch. But when wounded British soldiers had been brought to Beanes for care, he had treated them well. This was not a man who deserved to be held in the naval brig.

Cockburn promised to release Beanes the next morning. But Key and Beanes would have to spend the night on their boat amid the British fleet. It was too dangerous for them to return home now, as the British would be attacking Baltimore.

That night, Key watched the British rockets rip through the sky towards Fort McHenry, and the Americans respond with cannon fire. Through all the gun smoke, swaying above the fort, he saw one of the largest battle flags ever made, a star-spangled banner thirty-six feet long by twenty-nine feet wide. To distract himself from the fighting he pulled out his quill and wrote a poem to the tune of a bawdy British drinking song called "To Anacreon in Heaven." So that's a third thing to love about our anthem. The tune was made popular by a rowdy bunch of London ne'er-do-wells. This speaks well of our open-mindedness. It's usual to sing only the first verse, but to belt out all four gets the Fourth off to a suitably rousing start.

23

THE STAR-SPANGLED BANNER

BY FRANCIS SCOTT KEY, 1814

Oh, say can you see by the dawn's early light
What so proudly we hailed at the twilight's last gleaming?
Whose broad stripes and bright stars thru the perilous fight,
O'er the ramparts we watched were so gallantly streaming?
And the rocket's red glare, the bombs bursting in air,
Gave proof through the night that our flag was still there.
Oh, say does that star-spangled banner yet wave
O'er the land of the free and the home of the brave?

On the shore, dimly seen through the mists of the deep,
Where the foe's haughty host in dread silence reposes,
What is that which the breeze, o'er the towering steep,
As it fitfully blows, half conceals, half discloses?
Now it catches the gleam of the morning's first beam,
In full glory reflected now shines in the stream:
'Tis the star-spangled banner! Oh long may it wave
O'er the land of the free and the home of the brave!

And where is that band who so vauntingly swore
That the havoc of war and the battle's confusion,
A home and a country should leave us no more!
Their blood has washed out their foul footsteps' pollution.
No refuge could save the hireling and slave
From the terror of flight, or the gloom of the grave:
And the star-spangled banner in triumph doth wave
O'er the land of the free and the home of the brave!

Oh! thus be it ever, when freemen shall stand
Between their loved home and the war's desolation!
Blest with victory and peace, may the heav'n rescued land
Praise the Power that hath made and preserved us a nation.
Then conquer we must, when our cause it is just,
And this be our motto: "In God is our trust."
And the star-spangled banner in triumph shall wave
O'er the land of the free and the home of the brave!

Just as the mist is burning off the lake and we finish the last verse, the lumberjacks step out of the woods. These are tough men, silent and strong. Many are French Canadians who have made their lives in the Adirondacks, far from home. If you asked them, and they bothered to respond, they'd say Paul Bunyan was a wimp. An ax in their giant paws looks like a butter knife in yours or mine. It takes brute strength to fell an Adirondack spruce. But once cut, milled, and polished, the wood makes the finest pianos in the world. Today the lumberjacks scrub down, abandon their dusty encampments, and return to civilization for a few hours for Woodsman's Day. They compete in one-man sawing, crosscut sawing, chopping with axes, pulling logs, felling trees, and driving stakes into the ground. But the most popular event of all is the logrolling. The crowd roars as these mountain men move their feet like ballerinas to stay upright on the water-slick log. And when they fall, their legs apart . . . up goes a collective "*Yowch!!!*" Prizes are paid in cash and after a smoky meal, the woodsmen disappear again, for another year of quiet toil in the woods. These are not greedy men, but they are cutting down trees faster than they can grow back, at the cost of the Adirondacks' health. Soon they and their traditions will have to move on.

Last year, we erected a flagpole beside the house. It looks splendid and demands respect. The flag goes up in the morning and comes down at night. But you can't just bundle it up like a bedsheet. There are special rules about folding a flag. No part of it must touch the ground. It must be folded by two people into the shape of the three-cornered hats worn by the American soldiers who fought the War for Independence. As the flag is folded, the stripes disappear into the dark blue corner, symbolizing the light of day vanishing into the dark, starry night. We can be a little sloppy on Raquette Lake. But we do our best to stick to the rules laid out by the U.S. Air Force Academy:

The first fold of our flag is a symbol of life.

The second fold is a symbol of our belief in the eternal life.

The third fold is made in honor and remembrance of the veterans departing our ranks who gave a portion of life for the defense of our country to attain a peace throughout the world.

The fourth fold represents our weaker nature, for as American citizens trusting in God, we turn to Him in times of peace as well as in times of war for His divine guidance.

The fifth fold is a tribute to our country, for in the words of Stephen Decatur, "Our country, in dealing with other countries, may she always be right; but it is still our country, right or wrong."

The sixth fold is for where our hearts lie. It is with our hearts that we pledge allegiance to the flag of the United States of America, and to the republic for which it stands, one nation, under God, indivisible, with liberty and justice for all.

The seventh fold is a tribute to our Armed Forces, for it is through the Armed Forces that we protect our country and our flag against all her enemies, whether they be found within or without the boundaries of our republic.

The eighth fold is a tribute to the one who entered into the valley of the shadow of death, that we might see the light of day, and to honor mother, for whom it flies on Mother's Day.

The ninth fold is a tribute to womanhood, for it has been through their faith, love, loyalty and devotion that the character of the men and women who have made this country great has been molded.

The tenth fold is a tribute to father, for he, too, has given his sons and daughters for the defense of our country since they were first born.

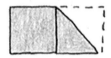

The eleventh fold, in the eyes of Hebrew citizens, represents the lower portion of the seal of King David and King Solomon, and glorifies, in their eyes, the God of Abraham, Isaac, and Jacob.

The twelfth fold, in the eyes of Christian citizens, represents an emblem of eternity and glorifies, in their eyes, God the Father, the Son, and the Holy Ghost.

When the flag is completely folded, the stars are uppermost, reminding us of our national motto, "In God We Trust."

After the flag is completely folded and tucked in, it takes on the appearance of a cocked hat, ever reminding us of the soldiers who served under General George Washington and the sailors and marines who served under Captain John Paul Jones who were followed by their comrades and shipmates in the Armed Forces of the United States, preserving for us the rights, privileges, and freedoms we enjoy today.

I guess everyone's entitled to celebrate the Fourth of July how they like. At Coney Island, New York, there's a hot dog eating contest at Nathan's on Surf Avenue. Whoever eats the most hot dogs in ten minutes wins. What could be more American than that? Except for years, it was a Japanese man, Takeru Kobayashi, who won. He had a special technique. For weeks before the tournament, he would expand his stomach by eating fibrous foods, like watermelon and cabbage, and drinking lots of water. He would exercise vigorously to reduce the fat around his waist, so his stomach could expand even more and he could eat more, faster. Once the contest started, he broke each frankfurter in two and popped both halves into his mouth at the same time. Then he dipped the buns into water or 7 UP to make them softer and easier to chew. As he ate, he wiggled around so the hot dogs would pack more tightly in his stomach and take up the least amount of room. This way, he could inhale fifty or more hot dogs in ten minutes, one every twelve seconds. I suggested to Dad we stage our own Hot Dog Guzzler up here at Raquette Lake, but he gave me the stink eye.

31

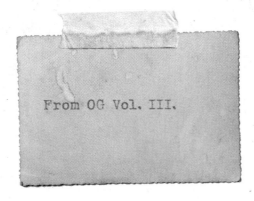

WHISTLER

September 15th, 1901
Gore Mountain Lodge
North Creek, New York

Dear Charlie,

I am sure the news has reached you by now, about our old friend Teddy. I know he is one of your favorite people. No one else causes quite the same rumpus when he visits us on Raquette Lake, knocking over the furniture and charming everyone in sight. And who brings better gifts? I'm thinking of your room and can see a rhinoceros horn from Africa on the shelf by the window, a mounted bonefish from Cuba on your dresser, and that bow and arrow from the Lakota. Don't think I've forgotten how you nearly killed your sister with that thing last summer. What were you thinking firing an arrow out over the lake without bothering to see if anyone was swimming? Of course, Teddy found that very funny, which I suppose is what makes him so appealing to boys. For all his success, he has never stopped being one himself.

I shall be home soon to talk about all of this in person. It's not every day a good friend becomes president of the United States. And we must

Theodore Roosevelt: Rumpus Causer

wish him the very best. But I thought I'd take the chance to scribble you a note about how it all happened.

Teddy had asked me to go with him and his family on a hike. You'll know from the newspapers about the appalling events a few days earlier in Buffalo. A maniac by the name of Leon Czolgosz had accosted President McKinley at the Pan American Exposition. He lurched up holding a revolver under a handkerchief he had made to look like a bandage. He shot the president once in the chest, and once in the stomach. Czolgosz was apprehended and the president taken into care. The initial prognosis was promising. It seemed McKinley would recover.

So Teddy had left his side and joined us up in this corner of the Adirondacks. But he was far from his usual, buoyant self.

From the moment he arrived, the news turned bad. A relay of runners, men on horseback, and telephone operators brought word of the president's worsening condition. Gangrene had set in. Teddy was facing the possibility of becoming president in the last way any man would want.

But he insisted, as usual, on exercise. And plenty of it. So off we went up Mount Marcy. I suggested a smaller peak. But no. Marcy it must be, the peak the Indian tribes called Cloudsplitter. On a fine day, there is no view to compare with the view from the top, all the way across our beloved Adirondacks. But in the pouring rain, it's nothing but mud and misery.

I've been Teddy's guide and companion several times in the Adirondacks and in many other places besides, from the empty lands of the West to the African bush. And I knew from experience that the moment you reacted to a challenge by saying, "We shouldn't," Teddy would respond, "Then we must!" It is his nature.

34

So we set off, the darkening skies matching the anxious mood of our party. Teddy and I walked together. There really is no one with a mind like his, with the sheer range of knowledge, interests, and enthusiasms. He has lived in one life what it would take an average man seven or eight lives to live. He has written books, traveled the world, been a war hero, learned European and Indian languages, studied botany, excelled at every sport from boxing to hunting, and still found time for politics. He once explained his attitude to life by quoting a line from an English poet, Thomas Mordaunt.

One crowded hour of glorious life
Is worth an age without a name.

To walk with him, even under such dismal circumstances, was an education. He pointed out animals and described trees and plants. Whenever the others had to stop, he would drag me off into the woods to listen to birdsong. I remember once losing him on a hike and finding he had gone and slung a rope over a branch and was hanging from it like an ape. He explained that he was trying to strengthen his wrists.

After a few hours, we stopped at Lake Tear-of-The-Clouds. Teddy marched off as usual, while I stayed with the group to make sure they were all right. As we sat beside the gray water, our old friend Harrison Hall came struggling out of the woods towards us. He was gasping for breath and his jacket was covered in briars and mud. He removed his hat and asked where he could find the vice president. Teddy was standing at the foot of a tree, his hand cupped around his ear, lost in the music of the forests.

"Beautiful!" he said. "Wood thrushes. We have them at home on

Long Island. They rouse us in the mornings and sing through the long summer afternoons."

"Mr. Vice President," said Hall, thrusting out a telegram. Teddy's face soured. He reached out and tore it open. He pushed his glasses up on his nose, and read. He gazed upwards again into the towering trees. The rain was falling in a fine spray.

"How soon before we can get back down?" he said.

"It's not safe in this weather," I said. Clouds were huddling over Mount Marcy. "We should get back to the camp and wait a few hours, to see if the weather clears."

He pressed the telegram into my hand as he strode past.

THE PRESIDENT IS CRITICALLY ILL
HIS CONDITION IS GRAVE
OXYGEN IS BEING GIVEN
ABSOLUTELY NO HOPE.

I followed Teddy back to his wife and children, who looked in need of a warm drink and a blazing fire. Without stopping, he led us back in the direction of the upper camp. He walked without saying a word. We hurried along behind him. On any other day, we would have descended the mountain in high spirits, ignoring the rain and looking forward to a fine dinner well earned. But today, we strode on in silence, the cold seeping into our bones.

After a couple of hours, we saw the camp. It was approaching nightfall.

"We shall spend the night here and go down in the morning," Teddy said, before retiring with his wife and children for dinner.

I had no appetite and paced up and down outside the cabin. It was nearly midnight when I heard a horse snorting up the path towards us. A messenger swung down from the saddle and rapped hard on the door of the vice president's cabin. Teddy appeared in the fire-lit doorway. The messenger handed him a telegram. Teddy opened it and nodded.

"I cannot wait any longer, Charlie," he said to me. "How long will it take to get to North Creek station? I can pick up a train there."

"In good weather, by daylight, it would take seven hours. At night, in this weather? Longer. If you can get there at all."

"I have no choice," he said. "If no one will take me, I shall walk." He handed me the telegram.

THE PRESIDENT APPEARS TO BE DYING AND MEMBERS OF THE CABINET IN BUFFALO THINK YOU SHOULD LOSE NO TIME COMING.

"You shall need fresh horses to break up the journey," I told the messenger. "You can ride the buck-wagon and horses we have down to the Tahawus Post Office. That's ten miles. Then you shall need to change again at Aiden Lair Lodge. Get word to Mike Cronin. He must help you down to North Creek."

The messenger climbed back on his horse, wheeled around, and galloped away. Teddy went back into the cabin. His children were fast asleep, but he kissed his wife, who was sitting up with him. I went and prepared the buck-wagon.

It seemed too basic a transport for a vice president of the United States on so important a mission. But it was all we had. I checked the wheels and axles. If the wagon were to break at any point on the journey, he might be stuck for hours in the cold and darkness.

"Hurry. Go Faster."

Teddy appeared outside in a borrowed raincoat, much too large for him, and a wide-brimmed slouch hat pulled down to just above his glasses. He climbed into the wagon's back seat and Jimmy, an experienced young driver, sat up front. Jimmy flicked the reins and surged into the darkness. A flickering lamp, which swung with the motion of the cart, was all he had for light. The last I saw of Teddy that night, he was swaddled in his raincoat, with water dripping from his hat brim. He seemed like an object carved from the New York earth, imperturbable and grave.

They plunged downwards, the buck-wagon jolting along beneath them, heaving and cracking. Deer leaped off the path and into the woods, startled by the sound of the wagon rattling down. One large rock in their path, and they would all be flung out. The wagon would splinter apart. On either side lay deathly falls, hundreds of feet straight down to rocks and bogs. To have lost one president, McKinley, so unexpectedly was a tragedy. To lose another in quick succession would have been a disaster.

At the Tahawus Post Office, two men waited in the rain with fresh horses and a new wagon.

On the next stage of his descent, Teddy began to murmur to himself. Over the sounds of slurping mud and splashing rain, he muttered "McKinley," and the name of the assassin, and suddenly, his face red and his breath hot, he lurched towards his driver and hissed: "If it had been I who had been shot, he wouldn't have got away so easily . . . I'd have guzzled him first."

It was another nine miles to Aiden Lair Lodge, the sportsmen's lodge in Minerva, and they arrived there shortly after 3:30 a.m. Mike Cronin, the lodge manager, was ready with his rig.

"Any news?" barked Teddy as he stepped down.

"Not a word," said Cronin. "Jump in right away and we'll be off." Cronin fumbled with his lamp and Teddy grabbed it from his hands and clambered up beside him. Cronin said his two black Morgan horses seemed to grasp the importance of their mission. Their eyes gleamed in the lamplight and they broke into a fast trot. They had been with Cronin for many years and knew these paths the way a priest knows his sacristy or a baseball player the lines and kinks of his home field.

They raced through narrow passes, and across bare hillsides. Their hooves struck sparks on hard rock. They sped through bogs, pulling the wagon as its wheels sank up to its axles in the unforgiving slime. When the horses stumbled, Cronin pulled back on the reins to slow them down.

"Push ahead!" cried Teddy. Cronin flicked them on with his whip. "Hurry, go faster," urged Teddy, peering into the darkness, willing it to part before him. Cronin told me he had never seen his horses work so hard. Steam billowed off their flanks. They took one corner so fast, one horse and half the wagon skidded out over a sheer drop, and the other horse had to yank them back in.

They crossed log bridges, which thrummed noisily beneath the hoofbeats, and passed a dance taking place in the light of a bonfire. As the wagon approached, the dancers, men and women, scampered guiltily into the woods. None could have known who it was gliding past in the darkness, but they ran as if it were the riders of the Apocalypse—or perhaps just the law. Shortly before dawn they clattered past a churchyard, its gravestones slick with rain, and Cronin turned to Teddy and said, "Just two miles to the station, sir."

"Well done," said Teddy. "Let's stop and let the horses blow."

The rain had stopped. Teddy removed his outsized raincoat. He smoothed out his tie and suit. He wanted to look presentable when he arrived at the station.

"Let us pray the president is still alive," he said.

The sun was now sweeping away the damp night, and the horses strode majestically over the last two miles. The cliffs along the rushing Hudson turned pink as they entered North Creek. The streets were still empty, the houses still dark. A small crowd of local politicians had gathered to meet the vice president. As Teddy approached, they cried, "There he comes!"

Behind them on the track, a special train was billowing smoke. The station clock read 5:22 a.m.

Teddy's secretary, William Loeb, removed his hat and, without saying a word, handed Teddy a telegram. It was from John Hay, the secretary of state, in Washington. Teddy unfolded the paper and read.

THE PRESIDENT DIED AT TWO-FIFTEEN THIS MORNING.

He had become president somewhere on the muddy path from the Tahawus Post Office to the Aiden Lair Lodge. He looked crestfallen for a moment. But breathed in, threw back his shoulders, and strode to the locomotive. He turned on the step and looked back. He waved to the crowd and disappeared.

Once, during a time of difficulty in my own life, when a venture had failed and I was feeling sorry for myself, Teddy wrote to me about the difference between those who act and those who sit on the margins, criticizing. I still have his letter somewhere, and I dig it out whenever I feel afraid of following my convictions. I found it again this morning.

41

"It is not the critic who counts," he wrote. "Not the man who points out how the strong man stumbles, or where the doer of deeds could have done them better. The credit belongs to the man who is actually in the arena, whose face is marred by dust and sweat and blood; who strives valiantly; who errs, and comes short again and again, because there is no effort without error and shortcoming; but who does actually strive to do the deeds; who knows the great enthusiasms, the great devotions; who spends himself in a worthy cause; who at the best knows in the end the triumph of high achievement, and who at the worst, if he fails, at least fails while daring greatly, so that his place shall never be with those cold and timid souls who know neither victory nor defeat."

I shall be home very soon and cannot wait to see you, Charlie.

Your loving father

In 1900, the first railway service began linking Raquette Lake to the New York Central Line, which clattered all the way down to Grand Central Terminal in Manhattan. It would have been of use to Theodore Roosevelt that night he became president. New Yorkers could now board a sleeper in the city and wake up a few hours later by the shores of Raquette Lake. The Whistlers were no longer quite so secluded as they were. The whole world was shrinking back then, as it still is. I found these next two pieces in OGs I and III.

43

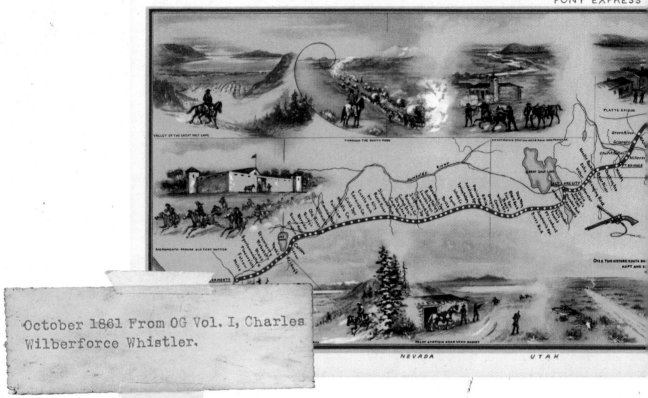

October 1861 From OG Vol. I, Charles Wilberforce Whistler.

WANTED: YOUNG, SKINNY, WIRY FELLOWS NOT OVER EIGHTEEN. MUST BE EXPERT RIDERS, WILLING TO RISK DEATH DAILY. ORPHANS PREFERRED. (Pony Express Poster)

The Pony Express has stopped service as it kept losing money. Shame. It offered tough, lucrative work for tough, quick boys. And a useful threat when any pampered young Whistlers stepped out of line. "Say that again, and you'll be riding the Pony Express!" It opened for business in April 1860 to allow

44

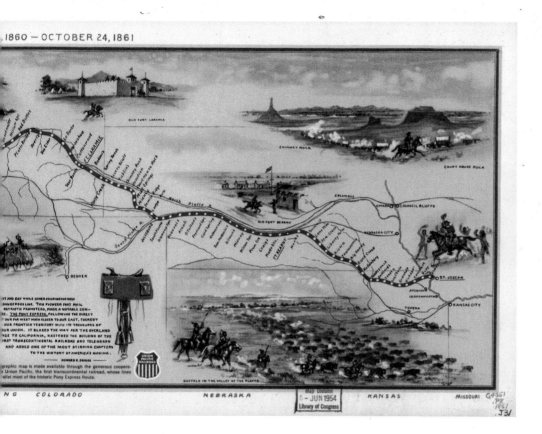

faster communication between the Eastern and Western states. The route from St. Joseph, Missouri, to Sacramento, California, ran 2,000 miles and could be covered in eleven and a half days by relays of horses and riders carrying saddlebags of mail through wild country. Despite all the dangers, they only ever lost one bag of mail.

February 23rd, 1921. (This was written by Charles Watson Whistler, a journalist who created the *Raquette Reporter* to occupy himself during the summers. He'd write up stories he'd covered for his work and then throw in reports of any local brouhahas and shenanigans to fill the pages. We've kept it going and when we can get organized, we send out a copy with our Christmas cards. I found this in Charles Watson's OG, Vol. III.)

THE RAQUETTE REPORTER

By Charlie Whistler

CHECKERBOARD FIELD, CHICAGO

All the fires of hell couldn't have warmed us up this morning, as we stood out on the airfield, peering into the sky for signs of Jack Knight and his De Havilland DH–4. And certainly not the lukewarm coffee served up by the Post Office, which had invited us reporters out here to witness this first transcontinental airmail service.

The Post Office wants the government to invest in an airmail system. So yesterday, Washington's Birthday, it sent two planes from San Francisco, California, to fly all the way to Long Island, New York, and two more to fly in the other direction.

Trains can now cross the country in 108 hours. The Post Office says its planes can do it in much less with its flying version of the Pony Express. The eastward flying route goes from San Francisco to Elko, Nevada, to Salt Lake City, Utah, then Cheyenne, Wyoming. From there, it's over to North Platte, Nebraska, along the route of the Union Pacific Railroad, then Omaha, Iowa City, Chicago, Cleveland, and finally New York.

But the planes they're using leave the pilots open to the weather, which in February in the Midwest is no joke. And what's more, the pilots have no way

to find the route at night. The solution to the cold is to dress up the pilots in layers and layers of waterproof leather, including face masks and goggles, with newspapers shoved down their jackets for extra warmth. As for the darkness, the Post Office has ordered its employees to line the route with bonfires lit inside used oil drums to show the pilots where to go.

We spent last night shivering in a metal hut close by the landing strip, here in Chicago. The news coming in along the route was bad. One of the planes flying east had crashed in Nevada and its pilot had been killed. The planes flying west were stuck in a snowstorm. Their mail had been unloaded and put onto trains. The officials from the Post Office were looking forlorn. All their hopes came down to one man, Jack Knight.

Knight had taken over one of the eastbound planes in North Platte. He followed the line of torches and bonfires all the way to Omaha, landing at 1:10 a.m. The pilot who was supposed to relieve him hadn't been able to leave Chicago because of the storm. Knight had never flown east of Omaha in his life, but after a cup of coffee, he climbed back into his cockpit and took off. Below him, postal workers and farmers tended their fires. He was meant to land in Des Moines, but the snow on the runway was too deep. So he pressed on to Iowa City, where a watchman lit a flare to illuminate the landing field. In high winds, Knight skidded in to land. After another brief rest, he took off into the mist for Chicago.

At 8:40 a.m., we heard a buzzing and saw Knight descending from the clouds. We cheered as he stepped out of his plane. He showed us the compass and torn road map he had used to navigate across 830 miles. Without the bonfires, he said, he would certainly have been lost. He pointed to the scar on his nose, where he had broken it a few days earlier. It hadn't yet healed fully and the cold and turbulence of the flight had been excruciating. At 9:00 a.m., the next pilot took off for Cleveland, and the plane finally arrived in New York at 4:50 that afternoon—2,629 miles had been covered in 33 hours and 20 minutes. Knight is an undisputed hero.

From OG Vol. VI, 2015.

If you visit the American Museum of Natural History in New York you are greeted by a statue of Theodore Roosevelt on horseback. Standing to either side of him are two guides, an American Indian and an African. The way he's thrusting out his chest, he looks like some ancient Roman general off to do battle. But pigeons would sit on his head and do what pigeons do, so the museum added spikes to the top of TR's head to put the birds off roosting there. When you actually go into the museum, there in the entrance hall are four enormous panels inscribed with his words. You can tell he was a remarkable guy. But to be his son, or even just his friend, and to have to live up to these standards. The pressure!

YOUTH

I want to see you game, boys. I want to see you brave and manly.
And I also want to see you gentle and tender.

Be practical as well as generous in your ideals and keep your eyes on the stars and keep your feet on the ground.

Courage, hard work, self-mastery and intelligent effort are all essential to a successful life.

Character in the long run is the decisive factor in the life of an individual and of nations alike.

NATURE

There is a delight in the hardy life of the open.

There are no words that can tell the hidden spirit of the wilderness that can reveal its mystery, its melancholy and its charm.

The nation behaves well if it treats the natural resources as assets which it must turn over to the next generation increased and not impaired in value.

Conservation means development as much as it does protection.

MANHOOD

A man's usefulness depends upon his living up to his ideals insofar as he can.

It is hard to fail but it is worse never to have tried to succeed.

All daring and courage, all iron endurance of misfortune make for a finer, nobler type of manhood.

Only those are fit to live who do not fear to die and none are fit to die who have shrunk from the joy of life and the duty of life.

THE STATE

Ours is a government of liberty by, through and under the law.

A great democracy must be progressive or it will soon cease to be great or a democracy.

Aggressive fighting for the right is the noblest sport the world affords.

In popular government, results worth having can only be achieved by men who combine worthy ideals with practical good sense.

If I must choose between righteousness and peace, I choose righteousness.

In ancient Athens, young men between the ages of 18 and 20, known as "ephebi," had to enroll for two years of military and civic training. After the first year, they were given a spear and shield and had to swear this wordy oath. I think President Roosevelt would have approved.

> I will not bring shame upon the sacred weapons nor desert my comrade, wherever I stand in the line. I will fight for things sacred and profane, and will pass on my fatherland greater than I found it, to the extent I can do so alone and with the help of others. I will obey the magistrates who rule with reason and I will observe the existing laws and any reasonable laws made in the future. If anyone seeks to overturn the laws, I will oppose him, either alone or with all to help me. I will honor the religion of my fathers. I call to witness the gods, Aglaurus, Hestia, Enyo, Enyalios, Ares and Athena Areia, Zeus, Thallo, Auxo, Hegemone, Heracles, and the borders of my fatherland, the wheat, the barley, the vines, olives, and figs.

If you found yourself in a fix in ancient Greece, you might visit the town of Delphi, where a priestess, called the Pythia, offered prophecies said to come from the god Apollo. On Apollo's temple were carved these words of advice: "Nothing in Excess" and "Know thyself." On these two principles of moderation and self-knowledge great lives can be built.

From OG Vol. III, 1905. No Whistler came down with the TR bug harder than Great-Grandfather Charles Watson Whistler. His OG is stuffed with notes like these.

HAY FOR THE HORSES

BY GARY SNYDER

He had driven half the night
From far down San Joaquin
Through Mariposa, up the
Dangerous Mountain roads,
And pulled in at eight a.m.
With his big truckload of hay
    behind the barn.
With winch and ropes and hooks
We stacked the bales up clean
To splintery redwood rafters
High in the dark, flecks of alfalfa
Whirling through shingle-cracks of light,
Itch of haydust in the
    sweaty shirt and shoes.
At lunchtime under Black oak
Out in the hot corral,
—The old mare nosing lunchpails,
Grasshoppers crackling in the weeds—
"I'm sixty-eight" he said,
"I first bucked hay when I was seventeen.
I thought, that day I started,
I sure would hate to do this all my life.
And dammit, that's just what
I've gone and done."

From OG Vol. IV, 1960.

Don't waste time

53

September 27th, 1909

WHISTLER

'Allo from Paris, mes chers Whistlers.

Fall here is not a patch on the Adirondacks. No forests or lakes or moaning loons. Just endless tree-lined boulevards and all the runny cheese a man can eat.

Today, I went to hear a talk given by an oddball named Jules Blois, who claims he can foresee the state of the world a hundred years from now. Women, he says, will be expected to be both muscular AND beautiful. No more delicate, lacy, fainting on the couch behavior will be accepted. We men will want our women hale, strong, and ready to stand beside us at the plow. Clearly this Blois hasn't spent much time with the women of Raquette Lake, otherwise he'd know the future was already upon us.

Motor cars will give way to flying bicycles. This seems a great shame, as I'm only just starting to enjoy motor cars. The faster and noisier the better. But in Blois's vision, we'll all be floating high above the earth on these contraptions, with no more need for roads.

Cities will become places for daytime business only. At night, everyone will hop on their flying bicycles, and head off to their homes in the country.

VOYAGE A LA LUNE.

Nations will no longer be ruled just by people with money or from powerful families. The new rulers will rise to the top based on their usefulness to society. This sounds the most sensible of Blois's ideas, though perhaps the most fantastical of all!

Alors, must run. Another giant meal awaits.

Au revoir,
Charlie

55

Fifty-five years later my
grandfather Charles Wilfred
Whistler took this note from
the newspaper and tucked it
into OG Vol. IV.

August 16, 1964

The World's Fair is afoot in Queens, New York, and in today's newspaper, the science fiction writer Isaac Asimov imagines visiting the World's Fair of 2014. Here's what he thinks the world will have by then:

- Electroluminescent wall panels that will change color at the press of a button.

- Polarized windows designed to keep out harsh light.

- Underground houses, with easily controlled temperatures and lighting. (Nature begone!!) Entire underground cities as the land aboveground is all needed for agriculture.

- Kitchen appliances which produce "automeals." Order your breakfast the night before and it'll be ready when you wake up.

- Robots able to do a few household tasks, like cleaning up and gardening.

- All appliances run on batteries. No more power cords!

- Solar power stations in space, collecting sunlight and beaming it down to Earth.

- Cars which travel on a cushion of air and never touch the ground. No more need for pavements or bridges.

- Driverless cars.

- Moving sidewalks to convey people around cities. Compressed air tubes to carry goods and materials around.

- Sight-sound telephones. You won't just hear the person you're calling, you'll be able to see them too.

- You'll be able to make telephone calls to people living in colonies on the Moon.

- 3-D television.

- Lots more people. The whole area from Boston to Washington, via New York, will have become a single 400-million-person city. The world's population will have doubled to 6.5 billion.

- Underwater housing serviced by "bathyscapes"—small submarines—going back and forth to the surface of the ocean.

- Algae Bars serving "mock turkey" and "pseudosteak."

The biggest problem he sees, aside from overcrowding, is that with all these machines doing so much for us, we'll all be bored out of our skulls. Instead of wanting a break from work, we'll be craving a break from too much leisure. Imagine that. Wanting to go to work, just to get away from all the darned thumb-twiddling.

January 1915

John Muir, the naturalist and author who did so much to preserve the wilderness of California, died over the Christmas holidays. He wrote that as children he and his friends had "wildness in our blood." I wish the same for every Whistler—young and old—in 1915 and beyond. May you all have wildness in your blood!

When I was a boy in Scotland I was fond of everything that was wild, and all my life I've been growing fonder and fonder of wild places and wild creatures. Fortunately around my native town of Dunbar, by the stormy North Sea, there was no lack of wildness, though most of the land lay in smooth cultivation. With red-blooded playmates, wild as myself, I loved to wander in the fields to hear the birds sing, and along the seashore to gaze and wonder at the shells and seaweeds, eels and crabs in the pools among the rocks when the tide was low; and best of all to watch the waves in awful storms thundering on the black headlands and craggy ruins of the old Dunbar Castle when the sea and the sky, the waves and the clouds, were mingled together as one. We never thought of playing truant, but after I was five or six years old I ran away to the seashore or the fields almost every Saturday, and every day in the school vacations except Sundays, though solemnly warned that I must play at home in the garden and back yard, lest I should learn to think bad thoughts and say bad words. All in vain. In spite of the sure sore punishments that followed like shadows, the natural inherited wildness in our blood ran true on its glorious course as invincible and unstoppable as stars.

John Muir

In Charles Wilfred Whistler's OG (Vol. IV), I found more on Muir. Charles Wilfred, my grandfather, was an avid hiker and once walked all the way from the Adirondacks down along the eastern coast to Florida. He wrote about Muir in his journal, copied out an extract from Muir's own writing.

May 1955. Charleston, South Carolina.

The more I learn about John Muir, the more I like him. At first, you see a photograph and think there was a bony, bearded, serious-looking fellow. The guardian of Yosemite and the Sierra Nevada. One of America's greatest environmentalists and the father of the National Parks. But he was also a tinkerer, a collector, and an adventurer. And funny to boot. As a teenager he loved building clocks and efficiency gadgets. He built a bed which would lurch upwards at a set time each morning, set him on his feet, and light a lamp. He devised a machine which held the books he had to read for school. A few minutes after he had been thrown out of bed, the first book would slide onto his desk and sit there for a fixed period of time before sliding away to be replaced by another. This was how he kept his homework organized.

When he was 29 years old, he walked a thousand miles from Indiana to the Gulf Coast of Florida, and through California, South America, the mountains of New England, scribbling in his notebooks. Here he is hailing a cabbage palmetto in Florida. He was reaching the end of his thousand-mile walk, and had found Florida inhospitable until he clapped eyes on this friendliest of trees. He dropped his bag and ran through marshy puddles to greet it. It seemed alive to him, human. A friend in an unfriendly place.

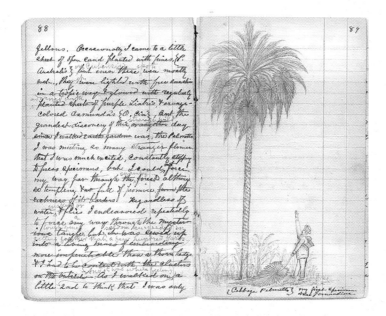

He believed that there were few things in life which could not be healed by Nature. "Keep close to Nature's Heart," he once said, "and break clear away once in a while and climb a mountain or spend a week in the woods. Wash your spirit clean." It's why we go to the Adirondacks and why I love to walk.

But if there is one image of Muir which has always stuck with me it's him climbing up a tree in a storm and relishing every sensation. People go to great lengths to excite themselves these days, from roller coasters to speedboats. But could anything be more thrilling than this?

FROM "A WIND-STORM IN THE FOREST"

One of the most beautiful and exhilarating storms I ever enjoyed in the Sierra occurred in December 1874, when I happened to be exploring one of the tributary valleys of the Yuba River. The sky and the ground and the trees had been thoroughly rain-washed and were dry again. The day was intensely pure, one of those incomparable bits of California winter, warm and balmy and full of white sparkling sunshine, redolent of all the purest influences of the spring, and at the same time enlivened with one of the most bracing wind-storms conceivable. Instead of camping out, as I usually do, I then chanced to be stopping at the house of a friend. But when the storm began to sound, I lost no time in pushing out into the woods to enjoy it. For on such occasions Nature has always something rare to show us, and the danger to life and limb is hardly greater than one would experience crouching deprecatingly beneath a roof. . . .

Toward midday, after a long, tingling scramble through copses of hazel and ceanothus, I gained the summit of the highest ridge in the neighborhood; and then it occurred to me that it would be a fine thing to climb one of the trees to obtain a wider outlook and get my ear close to the Æolian music of its topmost needles. But under the circumstances the choice of a tree was a serious matter. One whose instep was not very strong seemed in danger of being blown down, or of being struck by others in case they should fall; another was branchless to a considerable height above the ground, and at the same time too large to be grasped with arms and legs in climbing; while others were not favorably situated for clear views. After cautiously casting about, I made choice of the tallest of a group of Douglas Spruces that were growing close together like a tuft of grass, no one of which seemed likely to fall unless all the rest fell with it. Though comparatively young, they were about 100 feet high, and their lithe, brushy tops were rocking and swirling in wild ecstasy. Being accustomed to climb trees in making botanical studies, I experienced no difficulty in reaching the top of this one, and never before did I enjoy so noble an exhilaration of motion. The slender tops fairly flapped and swished in the passionate torrent, bending and swirling backward and forward, round and round, tracing indescribable combinations of vertical and horizontal curves, while I clung with muscles firm braced, like a bobo-link on a reed.

In its widest sweeps my tree-top described an arc of from twenty to thirty degrees, but I felt sure of its elastic temper, having seen others of the same species still more severely tried—bent almost to the ground indeed, in heavy snows—without breaking a fiber. I was therefore safe, and free to take the wind into my pulses and enjoy the excited forest from my superb outlook. . . .

Excepting only the shadows there was nothing somber in all this wild sea of pines. On the contrary, notwithstanding this was the winter season, the colors were remarkably beautiful. The shafts of the pine and libocedrus were brown and purple, and most of the foliage was well tinged with yellow; the laurel groves, with the pale undersides of their leaves turned upward, made masses of gray; and then there was many a dash of chocolate color from clumps of manzanita, and jet of vivid crimson from the bark of the madroños, while the ground on the hillsides, appearing here and there through openings between the groves, displayed masses of pale purple and brown.

The sounds of the storm corresponded gloriously with this wild exuberance of light and motion. The profound bass of the naked branches and boles booming like waterfalls; the quick, tense vibrations of the pine-needles, now rising to a shrill, whistling hiss, now falling to a silky murmur; the rustling of laurel groves in the dells, and the keen metallic click of leaf on leaf—all this was heard in easy analysis when the attention was calmly bent.

The varied gestures of the multitude were seen to fine advantage, so that one could recognize the different species at a distance of several miles by this means alone, as well as by their forms and colors, and the way they reflected the light. All seemed strong and comfortable, as if really enjoying the storm, while responding to its most enthusiastic greetings. We hear much nowadays concerning the universal struggle for existence, but no struggle in the common meaning of the word was manifest here; no recognition of danger by any tree; no deprecation; but rather an invincible gladness as remote from exultation as from fear.

I kept my lofty perch for hours, frequently closing my eyes to enjoy the music by itself, or to feast quietly on the delicious fragrance that was streaming past. The fragrance of the woods was less marked than

John Muir
up a Tree

that produced during warm rain, when so many balsamic buds and leaves are steeped like tea; but, from the chafing of resiny branches against each other, and the incessant attrition of myriads of needles, the gale was spiced to a very tonic degree. And besides the fragrance from these local sources there were traces of scents brought from afar. For this wind came first from the sea, rubbing against its fresh, briny waves, then distilled through the redwoods, threading rich ferny gulches, and spreading itself in broad undulating currents over many a flower-enameled ridge of the coast mountains, then across the golden plains, up the purple foot-hills, and into these piny woods with the varied incense gathered by the way. . . .

We all travel the milky way together, trees and men; but it never occurred to me until this storm-day, while swinging in the wind, that trees are travelers, in the ordinary sense. They make many journeys, not extensive ones, it is true; but our own little journeys, away and back again, are only little more than tree-wavings—many of them not so much.

When the storm began to abate, I dismounted and sauntered down through the calming woods. The storm-tones died away, and, turning toward the east, I beheld the countless hosts of the forests hushed and tranquil, towering above one another on the slopes of the hills like a devout audience. The setting sun filled them with amber light, and seemed to say, while they listened, "My peace I give unto you."

As I gazed on the impressive scene, all the so called ruin of the storm was forgotten, and never before did these noble woods appear so fresh, so joyous, so immortal.

Like Muir, Charles Wilfred Whistler was endlessly curious. Nothing was uninteresting to him. He made this collage to explain how the Greek scientist Eratosthenes had figured out the circumference of the Earth using nothing more complicated than a stick. Astronomers using satellite equipment recently measured the Earth's circumference at 40,008 kilometers, and its radius at 6,378, proving he and his stick were right. On the back of his collage, Charles Wilfred wrote: "The pencil chewers shall inherit the earth!"

In 200 B.C. the Greek mathematician and astronomer Eratosthenes struck upon a way to measure the circumference of the Earth. He knew that on a particular day in Cyene (or Syene), a city in Egypt, the sun would be directly overhead. He then set up a stick in Alexandria 5,000 stadia away (800–900 kilometers) on this day and measured the angle of the shadow that the sun formed at midday. It came to 7.2 degrees. Since there are 360 degrees in a circle, he worked out that 5,000 stadia must be equal to one fiftieth of the circumference of the Earth (360/7.2). He therefore suggested the Earth's circumference must be 250,000 stadia (40,000 to 46,000 kilometers).

From this, using the geometry of circles, we can calculate the Earth's radius:

$$C = 2\pi r$$
$$40,000/2\pi = r$$

Radius of the Earth = 6,380 km

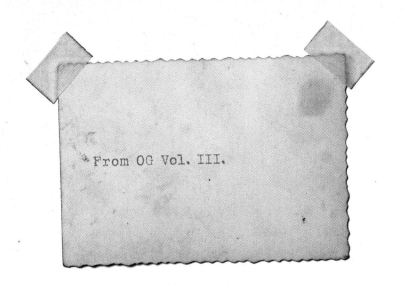

From OG Vol. III.

Written on the back of this photograph was:

"Go light, the lighter the better, so that you have the simplest material for health, comfort, and enjoyment."—Nessmuk

Nessmuk was the pen name of George Washington Sears, a 19th-century Adirondack guide.

Photograph by Basil Averathe

A PERSIAN BARBER IN GOOD HUMOR

As customers are only shaved about once a week, the clippers are first necessary. The hair of the head is also shaved from the forehead to the back.

HW

Mazar-e-Sharif, Afghanistan

Spring 1923

My Dear Kathleen—or I should say *Salaam Alaikum*—which means "greetings" in Pashto, the local tongue.

Now as you know, I'm not one to linger over a story. No point shilly-shallying, dilly-daddling, wiggle-waggling, or whiffling. No point at all. I see you in my mind's eye curled up in your bunk, the air cool and still outside. The reflections of the water shimmering on the ceiling. That worn red blanket, the color of prairie fire, keeping you warm. And I think to myself, Kathleen wants excitement! She craves the exotic! The sounds and smells of far-off lands. Drooling dromedaries and fabulous fakirs. Hissing cobras and eyeballs sizzling in fat—before being swallowed in one glutinous gulp.

Yes, I know what seizes the fancy of a young'un. For once, I was one too.

But today, I fear I must begin with a complaint. A croak from the sickbed. Unthinkable, I hear you cry. Not Uncle Henry. He who leaps into the frozen waters with nothing but the hair on his chest to keep him warm, and emerges singing the "Battle Hymn of the Republic." He who wrestles Kodiak bears with his bare hands. (Well, almost—no need to get persnickety about details. Oh fine, it wasn't a very big bear, and yes, I had a gun, but I did touch the thing once it was dead.)

But yes, I fear today, it is an enfeebled elder who writes to you, staving off the hard tackles of Infirmity with one hand, while scratching out this missive with the other. Yet, know this. My enfeeblement was in the noblest of causes. The preservation—and dare I say it—the burnishing of the Whistler name. Two cracked ribs, a flattened thumb, and a body aching from crown to heel are a small price to pay for the great victory scored on the plains of Mazar-e-Sharif today. The old Adirondack spirit shone through. And how!

I'm sure they're talking about it in the narrow streets of the town this evening, whispering and hollering from window to window, from shop to shop in the old bazaar, leaning their woolen caps in towards each other and murmuring in awestruck tones. Never in centuries, perhaps not since the Great Khan himself, the mighty Genghis, came thundering into town have they seen a foreigner triumph so completely in their midst.

But wait! I'm getting ahead of myself. The excitement is pumping through my brain and down to my one good hand, scribbling out the words before I can organize them into a proper yarn. Beginning, middle, and end as that wise Greek Aristotle used to say. That's what a story needs. So that's what you'll get.

As you know, work brought me to Afghanistan. Affairs of state, if you will. A reconnaissance on behalf of my superiors, that ramshackle band of botanists, cartographers, archaeologists, diplomats, and all-round busybodies in Washington, D.C., who insist on shunting me off to parts unknown in search of knowledge. Selfless to a fault, I packed the old camp bed and canvas shorts and away-ed. Weeks on the steamship ensued, with nothing to do for exercise but march in tedious circles around the decks, nodding at my fellow wanderers. We sailed through the Suez Canal, an eye-popping waterway linking the Mediterranean to the Red Sea, and thus West to East.

I would relate more of the passage, except I took in so little of it. Aside from pacing like a madman to keep the body in working order, I was heads-down in my cabin poring over the books. All of Europe and

Araby must have passed outside my porthole, but I paid not the slightest attention. My mind was focused on the journey ahead.

We were disgorged in the port of Karachi, a steamy entrepôt where even the sea seems to boil in the heat, and from here onto a caravan of worn-out jalopies for the journey north, to the Khyber Pass and then over into northern Afghanistan. We rattled our way across the country, our stomachs churning and our brains clattering around our skulls like dried peas in a can.

At the great Khyber, we transferred to horses, feisty beasts, muscled and harsh under saddle, but effective. They handled the rough paths as easily as you handle the toboggan run at Lake Placid. I thought of Alexander the Great astride Bucephalus passing through with his armies on his way to India. Dead at 30 after conquering most of the known world. Now there's a challenge for you, Kathleen.

This was where things got a little hairier. One night as we lay asleep, I heard a great commotion. I grabbed my pistol, pushed aside the flaps

of my tent, and strode out in nothing but my thick woolen underwear. Our guards were locked in battle with a band of ruffians. Fists were flying and I could make out the glint of blades. I determined to stop it and fired a shot in the air. The bandits turned and saw me and you'd think they'd seen Satan himself standing there in the amber light of the fire. Their eyes froze and their bodies quailed and they scattered like roaches into the darkness.

When they were gone, the guards looked at me and erupted in laughter. My first thought, I confess, was to consider them thankless curs. I had saved them from a night of savage fighting and all they could do was laugh. But when I caught sight of my reflection in the lid of one of our trunks, I understood. What a peculiar figure I must have seemed to them in my nightcap and underwear, my mustache oiled and packed tightly in its net, toting a gun. I could see the joke was on me—and it was a good one!

After several more days of hard riding, we reached our destination, the ancient town of Mazar-e-Sharif. The turquoise domes of the Shrine of Hazrat Ali, encircled by white pigeons, quickly made me forget my saddle sore rump. After so many hours of relentless brown landscape, just gazing upon the cool, blue tile was like a morning dip in Raquette Lake. Hazrat Ali was a cousin and son-in-law of Mohammed and he's said to be buried here. It's why the town bears the name it does: Tomb of the Exalted. Not a bad place to rest for eternity.

We clattered up to our home for the next few weeks, an old British fort on the edge of town, and while the others jostled for the best rooms, I plunked straight down onto a creaky old lounger in the hallway and fell asleep, snoring like a wildebeest, I imagine. (I've heard your impression of my snoring! Last summer, after Mrs. Evans's son Dwight performed

so poorly on his ukulele, you were up behind the boathouse with your cousins, thinking no one could hear you. . . .) But barely had my snores gained their beastly rhythm than I was roused. Looming over me was a turbaned face, creased, hook-nosed, and toothy.

"You are invited," he said.

"Invited to what?" I asked.

"To a contest." Now you know me, Kathleen. Like all Whistlers, nothing stirs the blood like a contest. Whether it's quarters, chess, or ski-jumping. Challenge a Whistler, I say, and reap the whirlwind!

"A contest of what?" I asked.

"Strength and courage," he said. He grinned and I could see the flash of several gold caps on his teeth. I stood up and realized he was as tall as me, dressed in loose pantaloons with a curved knife at his belt. An Afghan Whistler, perhaps.

"Lead on," I said. In uncertain situations, I've always found it helpful to jut out the chin, tighten the belt, and puff out the chest. Wherever you may be in the world, however different it may seem from what you are used to, men are men and women are women, and all respond to confidence, good cheer, and a proud bearing. Carrying yourself strongly packs a message in any language.

We walked a short distance to a large open space, mostly dirt but tufted with grass. A score of riderless horses frisked nervously around, as if being goaded by an invisible swarm of gnats. My guide walked me to a knot of men, dressed like him in baggy white pants, stout jackets, and turbans. Some wore handsome-looking hats, embroidered silk edged in fur. Each of them carried a short whip. As the men parted, they revealed a white stallion.

"We invite you to play Buzkashi," said my guide.

Now had I not spent my sea voyage reading up on the local culture, I should have been as bemused as you doubtless are now. "Buz-what-i?" But homework pays, Kathleen. I knew what I was in for. And there was no way out. My plan was to stay in Mazar-e-Sharif for months doing my fieldwork. If I flinched now, I would be known to these men as a weakling and coward. I swallowed hard and looked around.

The rules of Buzkashi are simple enough. The carcass of a calf is placed in the middle of the field. Then two teams of men on horseback hurtle towards it. The goal is to pick it up and hold on to it for an entire circuit of the field, and then drop it into a marked circle. The challenge is that as you ride at speed, your competitors will try to deprive you of the carcass by fair means or foul, shouting, pushing, and beating you with whips. It's rather like grabbing the last hot dog at the end-of-summer barbecue and trying to get it safely back to your room against the wishes of your grasping cousins.

The Afghans say Buzkashi is nothing more than the game of life played out on horseback. The goal is to grab the heavy prize, to endure the whips and blows of rivals, and heave it across the finish line.

The crowd bowed slightly and pointed towards the stallion. I gave them no hint of my reservations, but strode towards my steed and climbed aboard. He was all sinew and coiled energy, a rocket of a horse. I wheeled him around and the men scattered to their mounts.

A horn blew and the teams took up their positions. I took one last look around at the mountains and the piercing blue sky. I squinted to make out the carcass. My horse reared up slightly beneath me. And with another blast of the horn, we were off. An arm quickly shot out and struck me hard in the kidney. By the time I looked over to see the perpetrator, he was gone. So this was how it was going to be.

I dug my heels into my horse's flanks and urged him on. Dirt flew up into my eyes and on every side men jostled and pushed, seeking to push each other to the ground, where they would be kicked by the galloping horses. Up ahead, I could see we were nearing the carcass. A man in a crimson hat, the color of fresh blood, was reaching down, his body perpendicular to the ground. But just as he did so, another rider clattered in from behind, knocking him flat against his horse's neck. The man clung on tightly, his nose crushed into his face, as his horse wheeled away.

To my right, another rider, tall in the saddle and wearing a cloak trimmed in silver, reached up with his arm, letting his sleeve fall to his elbow, readying himself to swing down. Other men were leaning forward and out, their whips clenched between their teeth. I made a sudden decision to pull back. There was no use me diving into this donnybrook. Instead I slowed down and pulled around, out to the right of the pack. I feinted. Whoever hauled up the calf would have to emerge from the ruckus at some point.

I slowed down my nag and waited. Caterwauls and steam rose from the violent rumpus. I could hear the thwack of whips on skulls and the cries of pain. It was lucky the poor calf was dead already, because that would have been a hideous way to go. I waited. I could see the horses tiring as they were jostled. Suddenly a path opened up in front of me, and out popped my pal with the silver-trimmed robe. Blood was streaming from one of his ears and from a broad cut across his brow.

The carcass was draped across the neck of his horse like a cushion. He swatted back two riders, with a fist to the right and a flick of his whip to the left, and then he spurred on his horse. I turned sharply and rode up alongside him. He was leaning low over his trophy, his eyes narrowed and focused on the white circle still several hundred feet ahead.

We were both hurtling forward. I reached over and grabbed at the calf. He tilted away and the tips of my fingers grazed the slick hide. As he came upright again, I struck at his right hand, which was clutching his reins. He glared at me, a look of pure malice. We were close enough, I could see the red capillaries in his eyes, and they seemed to throb with hatred. He took the whip from between his teeth and began to strike me repeatedly. Each time I tried to land a blow in return, he struck me again. I lunged low to the right, away from his reach, and he seized the opportunity to gallop ahead. By the time I was upright again, he had put several feet between us.

I urged on my horse. My breath was short and my ribs were aching. The finish was fast approaching. Behind me, I could hear the snorts and cries of the other riders, closing in on us. The rider with the carcass pressed ahead, without looking back. I turned my horse to come in on his left side. As I came close, I reached forward with my stronger right arm and pulled at his robe, just above his waist. He turned and tried to strike me, but I was lying low and he couldn't twist his body enough to reach me. I pulled again, this time balling up the robe in my fist and I pulled him up and back. He was straining on the reins and his horse started to slow. As I came level with the rider, I jabbed him just below the rib cage, then shoved him so that his body toppled over, as his feet stayed in their stirrups. At the same moment I kicked at my horse and he accelerated. As I shot forward I grabbed at the carcass. I could feel my shoulder popping from its socket as I heaved it over towards my horse. It was as heavy as a bag of grain, but slippery to boot. I could feel it sliding through my fingers, pulling me downwards. It was like trying to hold on to a drowning man in a storm. You pull and strain to save his life, but his hand keeps slipping away.

The finishing circle was close now, less than 100 yards. But every yard was agony. And then I felt a bump. I could barely turn my neck as I was drooped over the side of the horse clutching the carcass. But then another one. My horse kept running. Another bump, this one more powerful. My horse lurched forward, his feet stumbling on the rough ground. The carcass slipped in my hand yet again. I had barely a palmful of it now and it brushed against the ground as we went, slowing us down even further. Then a sharp blow against my neck. The hooves of another horse were now rising and falling close to my face. Another blow struck my ear, like a slap to the face on a cold day.

Just a few more feet. I could smell the riders around me, the sweat of their horses, the blood and dirt caking their clothes. I could see the silver trim of my rival's cloak. A hoof struck the back of my head. My neck snapped forwards. My boots were sliding from their stirrups, my legs losing the strength to grip the horse. I was slipping down towards the ground where I would be trampled to death.

The blows were unremitting, slicing whips and solid thwacks. They came down on me from all sides. And then, I could hold on no more. My eyes turned dark and my body slumped forward and struck the ground. The horse ran off with one of my boots still in the stirrup.

I have no idea how long I lay there, but it cannot have been more than a few seconds. Because when I awoke, I was lying flat on my back, the carcass across my chest. All around me were the horsemen, holding their whips aloft. One of them let out a cheer, and the rest soon followed. The rider in the silver-trimmed robe was standing over me. He smiled and stretched out his hand. As I grabbed it, pain shot all over my body. But I managed to get to my feet. He then pointed to the ground. I had landed in the middle of the white circle. I held up the carcass, and the men cheered again, their voices carrying far in the thin mountain air, up towards the Hindu Kush.

Now does that explain my aches and pains? Do you forgive me now my earlier moment of self-pity? I do hope so.

But now I must scrub up and dress for dinner. The local elders have invited me to dinner. After a good game of Buzkashi, they roast the carcass used during the game, and serve the choicest morsels to the victor. I don't think I've ever had to work so hard for a meal.

And do you know what they call a Buzkashi champion, Kathleen?
A Chapandaz.

Your loving uncle,
Henry "Chapandaz" Whistler

(Call me anything else, and I'll beat you with a whip and pilfer your carcass!)

83

THE RAQUETTE REPORTER

Summer 1931

Boys in the Adirondacks have been building diving helmets to see how far down they can descend into our lakes. The *Schenectady Gazette* reports on one Harry K. Summerhayes, who has made a helmet which allows him to go down to 40 feet. He has even rigged up a telephone line so he can communicate with his friends on the surface. Another, Richard Garrett of Glens Falls High School, has been diving in Lake George using a helmet made out of a five-gallon oil can with two glass panels for viewing. He also ran a pipe into the helmet so air could be pumped down with a bicycle pump.

Their inspirations are William Beebe, a naturalist at the New York Zoological Society, and Otis Barton, an engineer. These two pioneers are so fascinated by the prospect of the ocean deeps that they have built themselves a bathysphere, a two-ton vessel the size of a wrecking ball, which can be lowered on a steel cable to a depth of half a mile. Recently, they took their curious craft for a spin near the island of Bermuda, and wrote up their experience for *National Geographic*.

As they passed 600 feet below sea level Beebe reflected that thousands of human beings had been down this far over the centuries—but all had been drowned. The slightest crack in the bathysphere, and they too would have been crushed to a pulp. At 800 feet, he and Barton saw lantern fish and hatchetfish blazing in the blue, platoons of flying snails and squid suspended in the water, barely moving their arms, like old men doing the backstroke. At 1,400 feet the bathysphere stopped. Beebe pressed his face against the window, and saw endless shades of blue, from the darkest blue surrounding them to the pale blue of the surface, and fish of the most brilliant colors. He wrote of that moment:

There came to me at that instant
a tremendous wave of emotion,
a real appreciation of what was
momentarily almost superhuman,
cosmic, of the whole situation; our
barge slowly rolling high overhead
in the blazing sunlight, like the
merest chip of the ocean, the long
web of cable leading down through
the spectrum to our lonely sphere,

where, sealed tight, two conscious human beings sat and peered into the abysmal darkness as we dangled in mid-water, isolated as a lost planet in outermost space. ("A Round Trip to Davy Jones' Locker," *National Geographic*, June 1931.)

Perhaps the boys groping through the gloom at the bottom of Lake George are experiencing similar emotions, but so far all that has been reported is that they have recovered an outboard motor.

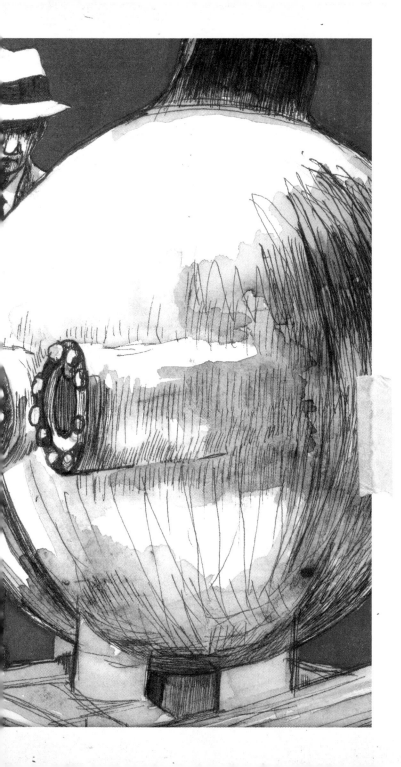

From OG Vol. VI, 2015.

Way out west in the northern Pacific Ocean, between Hawaii and China, is the Mariana Trench. To get to it, you go down, down, keep going down and then once you're as deep as you dare go, keep going. The trench is more than one and a half thousand miles long and about 40 miles wide, though it widens and narrows along the way. Scientists have been trying to measure its depths forever, but it's not easy. They send down electronic equipment only to find yet more trenches within the trench, and gullies, and holes. The deepest point found so far is Sirena Deep, a hole which bottoms out 35,000 feet or so below sea level. It takes a special kind of person to want to go down there. The film director James Cameron is one such deep-sea fanatic. He has designed and built his own submersible, *Deepsea Challenger*. In March 2012, he descended 35,756 feet, nearly 7 miles. When he came back up, he reported that it was extremely dark that far down, and that it felt like going to another planet and coming back—all in the space of a day.

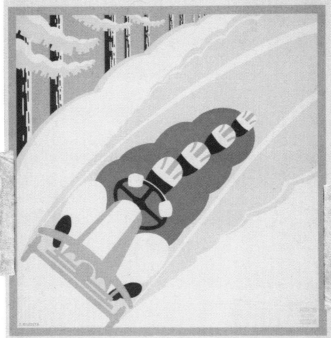

UP WHERE WINTER
≈ CALLS TO PLAY ≈

OLYMPIC
BOBSLED RUN
OPERATED BY N.Y. STATE CONSERVATION DEPT.
LAKE PLACID

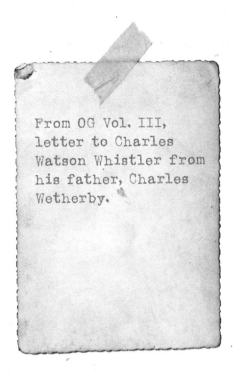

From OG Vol. III, letter to Charles Watson Whistler from his father, Charles Wetherby.

February 1932

Dear Charlie,

It's a shame you have to be all the way out in California and missing these Winter Olympics taking place right in our backyard, at Lake Placid. The town has been taken over by 231 men and 22 women, all rosy-cheeked and strong-limbed. They have come from 17 nations to compete in 14 contests in 5 different sports: bobsled, figure skating, Nordic skiing, ice hockey, and speed skating. You would have loved the carnival atmosphere.

You doubtless know all this, but I've been reading up on the history of these games. I thought they'd been around forever. I knew the ancient Greeks had created them and invited men, and men only, to travel to Olympia in the western Peloponnese every four years, slather their bodies in oil, and race and wrestle in honor of the gods. What I didn't realize was that shortly before A.D. 400, the killjoy Roman emperors, who had just become Christian, banned the games on the grounds that they were "pagan." It was another fifteen hundred years before a Frenchman, Baron de Coubertin, revived them. He held the first summer games in 1896 and the first winter games in 1924. The papers have been full of stories about this high-minded baron. He was determined that his games not be all about winning and losing and wrote that "the most important thing in the Olympic Games is not to win but to take part, just as the most important thing in life is not the triumph but the struggle, the essential thing is not to have conquered but to have fought well." Amen to that. For his symbol, the baron chose five interlocking rings. They represent Europe, Africa, Asia, Australia, and the Americas. Every national flag in the world has at least one of the colors represented in the rings: blue, black, red, yellow, and green.

The star of the games so far has been the American Eddie Eagan, a strapping man from Denver, Colorado, who became the only man to win gold in both the summer and the winter games. In 1920, he won gold in light-heavyweight boxing. In these games, he was part of the victorious American bobsleigh crew. Though the way he described coming down the run at 60 miles per hour, you felt he'd have rather taken a beating in the ring. "Just picture a steel comet with four riders hurtling through the air," he said after his race. The winning run took just two minutes, but Eagan said, "To me it seemed like an eon. I remember the snow-covered ground flashing by like a motion picture out of focus. Speeding only a few inches from the ground without any sense of security, I hung on to the straps. My hands seemed to be slipping, but still I clung."

The highlight for us locals has been once the Olympic races are over, when a few of us have been allowed to take a spin down the bobsleigh

track to see for ourselves what Eagan was talking about. It's a mile from top to bottom. One person sits up front and drives, and the other gives it an almighty push at the start, then jumps aboard and holds on all the way down. There's really no thrill like it. Half a ton of metal going downhill at sixty miles an hour. Chips of ice flying up into your face. I've enclosed a photograph of our amateur group to amuse you. No Eddie Eagans us!

At every turn, you have a choice to go high up the bank or stay down in the chute. The higher you go, the faster you go and the greater your chance of flipping the sled and sliding down the rest of the run on your head. When you reach the bottom, you hit the brake, screech, bounce against the walls of the run, take a breath, and realize how tense you've been the last 60 seconds.

If you're lucky, there's a truck waiting for you and a driver leaning out of the window saying, "Let's throw your sled in the back! There's time for one more run before it gets dark."

The reporters who have traveled to Lake Placid seem to find us a curious lot given to craziness on snow and ice. A man from the *New York Times* saw some local boys ski jumping, the way you used to, and wrote: "The winter afternoons of an American boy who is interested in ski jumping are different from those of his friends who are interested in, say, baseball. For one thing, young baseball players do not have to build a field." This past winter, a group of boys built a jump on top of the local movie theater, high enough so they could fly clear over Main Street and land in a parking lot on the other side.

A friend who knew this reporter asked if I could teach him to jump. I'm not the limber young buck of yesteryear, as you know, but I could scarcely turn down this chance. I began by taking him up one of the small jumps. We sat at the top and I could feel him trembling as he looked down. I gave him the usual spiel. Push off, crouch low, and bend forward to minimize wind resistance. When you hit the takeoff point, lean forward as far as you can, almost touching your skis with your nose as you rocket forward into thin air. I could tell from the way he looked at me that he trusted me about as much as I trust the bookmakers at Saratoga Springs.

I explained that he should try to lean his body at a 32-degree angle from the skis, so he might catch an updraft from the bottom of the hill and stay airborne a little longer. Push the skis too low and he would fall

too soon. He wanted to soar through the air like the wing of an airplane. He'd know if it was a "quiet one," a good jump, if his body remained still, and all he heard was the wind whistling past his ears. He pulled a flask from his jacket pocket and took a long swig.

I said he should try to land as late as possible, his knees bent, one leg in front of the other, arms out for balance, torso straight. I pointed out the two markers in the landing area: P marking the distance a good jumper is expected to jump; K about 15 to 20 meters farther on, represents the "critical point." If he soared past here, I warned him, he would have "out-jumped" and would be in serious danger of crashing into people, buildings, and anything else littering the bottom of a mountain. He gulped and before I could say anything else, tucked his hands behind his back and pushed off. He bent low, his skis fell into the grooves down the jump. He flew off the end, pulled up his skis, and began to flail. He windmilled his arms like a man trying not to fall backwards off a ledge. I heard a gasp from the crowd below. Twenty feet beyond the end of the jump, this estimable scribe thudded to the ground, rear first, back next, head last, and slid ignominiously down. When he came to a stop, he yanked off his skis and marched off towards the bar without so much as a thank-you.

I'm only glad we didn't try the ingrate out on the bobsleigh.

With love,
Your father

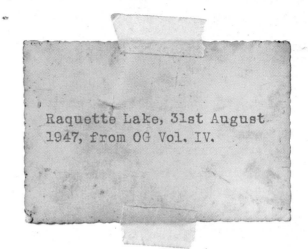

Raquette Lake, 31st August 1947, from OG Vol. IV.

THE RAQUETTE REPORTER

BY CHARLES WHISTLER,
SPECIAL CORRESPONDENT AND JOHNNY-ON-THE-SPOT

Four boys, ranging from the dumb to the downright idiotic, learned their lesson the hard way last night. Indian Pass is no place for the unprepared. This gloomy chasm must be respected or else it will swallow you whole.

I know, because I was one of them.

You spend enough years in the Adirondacks and you think you know them. You stop respecting these forests and mountains. You climb the 46 High Peaks and get the badge and you think that's that. And that is when bad things happen. I've lost count of the number of times I've been told this by senior Whistlers. "Respect the wilderness," they'd tell me. "Yeah, yeah," I'd say, and forget.

But you know what else they'd tell me? "There's no teacher like experience." And about that, they were absolutely right. You can read about fear, or hear about it. But there's nothing like feeling

SPOT THE FROGMAN.

its clammy fingers close around your heart to make you pay attention.

My friends and I had had a good morning of summer fun. Fishing off a boat, catching a few, missing many more, swimming, and racing our bikes round the dirt path circling the lake.

After lunch, we set out from the Adirondack Lodge for a hike, our bellies full of chili and sponge cake, wearing just shorts and summer shirts. "See you later," we yelled back as we made for the path leading out to the pass. Soon, we got to spooking each other and setting dares. You know the kind. Running ahead, lying in wait, and then leaping out from behind rocks and trees screaming "Woo-hoo!"

Without knowing it, we were waking the forest's malevolent ghosts.

When we arrived at Indian Pass, we gathered at the foot of Wallface, a vertical rock face rising more than 1,000 feet. It is where the men in town gather for bonfires and secret meetings. They said it was where the sprits of the Adirondack forests made their home. We stood for a while in silent awe, oblivious to the lengthening shadows. Then I whispered to my friends: "Bet you can't climb it."

In the mood we were in, it was impossible to resist. One by one, we started to scramble, making handholds of the tiniest cracks and dragging our bodies upwards—20, 30, 50, 60 feet up and up we slithered, our faces and bodies pressed to the cold rock, not thinking for a moment of the time or how we would ever get down.

Only one of us was sensible enough to stay on the ground. My 8-year-old cousin Alfred. Always a wise soul, he never seemed wiser, standing at the foot of Wallface, his head tilted sideways, baffled by our teenage shenanigans.

After 45 minutes of hard climbing, the three of us reached a narrow ledge. It was just two feet wide and sloping downwards at a 45-degree angle. We were desperate to rest, but as we looked around, we could see it was getting dark. The ledge could barely hold us. Just as we settled and found a shaky grip, a large chunk of rock crumbled and fell away beneath us. All we could do was hold on where we were.

"Alfie," I shouted down to my cousin. "Run back to the lodge and get help!"

"I don't know the way," he yelled.

"Follow our tracks. Just run." My

voice echoed back. I could just make out Alfred scrambling over the rocks. He was whimpering. I could understand. It was scary down there.

We clung on where we were. Our palms were sweating and slipping against the stone. The wind was starting to pick up and the air was turning cold as the devil.

"Whose dumb idea was this?" I said. Nobody answered. I could see my friends were as scared as me, and not in any mood for jokes. I wasn't either. But I thought we could use the distraction. I started to count. One Mississippi. Two Mississippi.

"Shut up," said Augie, who was the oldest of us at 16. "I can't move my fingers." I glanced down. His hand was clutching the rock as tightly as a claw. A cold wind was blowing straight into our faces and making my eyes tear up. Fog began creeping up through the pass just as the last daylight vanished. We couldn't see more than a couple of feet in any direction. We were marooned. One slip and we'd be dead. We could hear the sounds of the forest, the drip of water, our own breathing, the wind rushing through the trees. But it was all muffled by the thickening fog. I had

no idea what time it was, but I knew that my muscles were aching more with every second that passed.

"Fog means it's going to rain tomorrow," said Augie. "They'll never find us."

The ghosts of Indian Pass were at work.

Then through the gloom we heard a shout.

"Charlie! Charlie! Are you still there!" It was Alfie. I've never been so happy to hear him in my life, and promised right then never to steal his candy or lock him in cupboards again.

"Yes! We haven't moved," I shouted back. We could see the orange glow of torches, and more voices, adult voices. The moisture was turning to ice on the rock behind us.

"It's Jed Rosman here, Charlie." Jed is the caretaker of the lodge. No one knows these mountains better than Jed. "We're not going to be able to get to you today. You're just going to have to hold on. Tie yourselves together if you have to. We'll try first thing in the morning. Don't, whatever you do, try to get down." Fat chance. It was a straight drop 50 feet down to jagged rocks.

I turned to Augie, who turned to

Will, the third member of our group.

"Let's see if we can tie our belts together," I said. Will and Augie unbuckled their belts with one hand, while they held on to the rock with the other. We interlaced our three belts, wove them around our ankles, and pulled the final buckle tight around the exposed roots of a scraggly little bush, which had somehow seeded itself and grown on the ledge. We pushed ourselves as far back as we could, trying to burrow into what little shelter the ledge provided, and staying close to each other for warmth. We began to smell smoke and could see the sparks of a bonfire far below us, and the light flickering on the rock face opposite. It was hard to remain steady. Our legs grew sore from squatting and our feet ached from trying not to slip. None of us got a wink of sleep. The hours passed slowly.

I've never been so happy to see the morning light. The moment the blackness shaded to gray, we heard the rescue party start to move. At the count of three, we pushed ourselves up and shook out the cramps in our legs. Our faces and hands were frozen near solid.

The rescue party broke into two groups. One climbed Wallface from the rear. The other climbed McIntyre Mountain, opposite us, so they could see where we were. When the group on Wallface reached the summit, they lowered a parcel of food down on a rope. The rope kept getting tangled on rocks and we couldn't reach it. Eventually, they managed to dangle it out in front of us. I reached out and hauled it in. But as I did, several small rocks slipped out from under my feet. I was saved by the belt around my ankles and Will holding my hand. There were sardine sandwiches and an orange, which we gobbled down. I don't think anyone has ever enjoyed a sardine sandwich more than us that morning.

While we ate as fast as our frozen jaws allowed us, we heard a plane buzzing towards us. It was Fred McLane, a pilot we all knew from Lake Placid airport. He descended into the pass and switched off his engines so we could hear him as he shouted, "How ya' doing?"

"We're alive!" I shouted back. He gave us the thumbs-up, turned his engines back on, and soared up and away.

The Wallface party dropped another rope down and yelled down for us to grab it. Augie pulled it in.

"Tie it round your waist and we'll pull you up!"

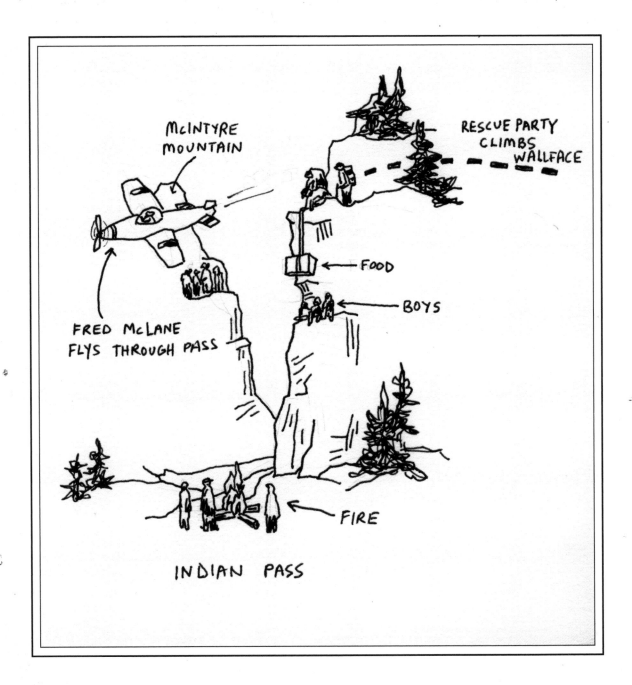

"You first," said Augie, handing it to me. "It was your idea to climb up here."

I took the rope and tied it tight, through my legs and around my waist.

"OK! Pull!" I shouted. I felt a sharp tug. Suddenly, my feet were off the ledge and dangling in thin air. I inched up a little before I felt the rope catch somewhere higher up. I inched back down again. This was going to take a while. I shut my eyes, breathed, and tried to forget where I was. It didn't work. The moment I opened my eyes and looked down, I felt a jolt of terror.

"We're going to lower you back down," said Jed Rosman's voice from above me. "This rope isn't strong enough." I tiptoed slowly back onto the ledge and Augie and Will helped untie me.

"Have a slice of orange," said Will. Its juice felt delicious on my dried throat.

The fog had cleared now and we could see all the way down into the pass. With a monstrous growl, three trucks heaved their way into the clearing next to Wallface. We could see all kinds of men now pouring out with ropes, ladders, axes, and helmets. A group of them stood with their hands on their hips looking up and shaking their heads.

"Are you there, boys?" We looked up and saw a pair of climbing boots dangling just a few feet above us.

"Down here!" we all yelled.

It was George Reynolds. If you ever find yourself in a situation like this, just hope there's a George Reynolds around to help out. He was a football star at college, and as strong as a bison.

"Now, how on earth did you get yourself into all this?" he said, smiling. "Get any sleep?" We shook our heads.

"Thought not. Now let's see if we can't get you back to your mothers. Throw down another rope!" he yelled, then turned back to us. "There's more of us up there now, and we've got a stronger rope."

As the second rope came down, he showed us how to tie it, making nooses under our armpits. Will went first, then Augie, then me. It took just half an hour to get the three of us up to safety.

We lay like basking seals on the wet rock at the top of Wallface. Our faces were white, near blue, our legs raw from exposure to the Adirondack night.

"Give them some coffee," Reynolds ordered. "Anything hot. And what have we got to eat?" We nursed the hot coffee and devoured a chocolate bar and more sandwiches. After about half an hour, we were ready for the walk back to the lodge.

103

Alfie joined us at the bottom of the pass. I gave him a hug.

"Anything you want, boy. It's yours," I said.

"How about your miniature sailing boat?"

"Not so fast!"

"You did say anything."

"Well, I guess you did save my life."

"A small price to pay."

The kid has the Whistler spirit.

I learned two things. If people say a place is haunted, don't get clever. Believe them.

And never go climbing without a rope, thick clothes, and friends who know what they're doing.

Never join a camping party that has among its members a single peevish, irritable, or selfish person, or a "shirk." Although the company of such a boy may be only slightly annoying at school or upon the playground, in camp the companionship of a fellow of this description becomes unbearable. Even if the game fill the woods and the waters are alive with fish, an irritable or selfish companion will spoil all the fun and take the sunshine out of the brightest day. The whole party should be composed of fellows who are willing to take things as they come and make the best of everything. With such companions, there is no such thing as "bad luck"; rain or shine everything is always jolly, and when you return from the woods, strengthened in mind and body, you will always remember with pleasure your camping experience.

The second was a curious collage (overleaf) with a scribble on one side explaining why we can see the moon during the day. I guess fearing for his life made him want to learn more about the workings of the world.

The moon does not radiate light the way the sun does. When you look at the moon, you are simply seeing the sun's light reflected off it.

Even though the moon is about as reflective as a road, the sun is so bright that its light reflected off the moon is still about 100,000 times as bright as the brightest star in the night sky.

During the day, the sunlit sky washes out the light from the stars, so you cannot see them. But because the moon is so much closer, you can often still see it even in daylight. You can also sometimes see Venus, if you know where to look, but any more distant stars become invisible.

You can think of the sun as a lightbulb and the moon as a mirror. At night, when we are facing away from the sun, we see the sun's light reflected off the moon. During the day, we can sometimes see both the bulb itself and its reflection in the mirror of the moon.

Charles Wilfred added this mnemonic to remember the planets in order of distance from the sun:

Men Very Easily Make Jugs Serving Useful Necessary Purposes.

Mercury, Venus, Earth, Mars, Jupiter, Saturn, Uranus, Neptune, Pluto.

(From OG Vol. VI, 2015: Pluto has been on then off this list as scientists keep haggling over whether or not it's a real planet. Right now they're calling it a dwarf planet, which seems kind of rude, but better than not being a planet at all.)

To become an Adirondack 46er and earn this handsome badge, you must climb all 46 of the Adirondacks' High Peaks. Some do it in a season, others take 30 years. Some like to climb the peaks in the summer, and then climb again in the winter, to experience the different conditions of heat, snow, and ice. The Adirondack 46 are:

RANKING IN HEIGHT	ELEVATION (FEET)	LENGTH OF ROUND-TRIP (MILES)	TYPICAL HIKE TIME (HOURS)
MT. MARCY	5,344	14.8	10
ALGONQUIN PEAK	5,114	9.6	9
MT. HAYSTACK	4,960	17.8	12
MT. SKYLIGHT	4,926	17.9	15
WHITEFACE MTN.	4,867	10.4	8.5
DIX MTN.	4,857	13.2	10
IROQUOIS PEAK	4,843	11.6	8.5
GRAY PEAK	4,840	16	14
BASIN MTN.	4,826	16.5	11
GOTHICS	4,734	10	9
MT. COLDEN	4,713	15.2	10
GIANT MTN.	4,622	6	7.5
NIPPLETOP	4,620	12.6	10
SANTANONI PEAK	4,607	11.4	10
MT. REDFIELD	4,606	17.5	14
WRIGHT PEAK	4,587	7	7
SADDLEBACK MTN.	4,530	13.4	10
PANTHER PEAK	4,448	17.6	13.5
TABLETOP MTN.	4,440	15.2	13
ROCKY PEAK RIDGE	4,390	13.4	11

MACOMB MTN.	4,371	8.4	8
ARMSTRONG MTN.	4,446	12.7	11
HOUGH PEAK	4,409	13.7	11
SEWARD MTN.	4,404	16	17
MT. MARSHALL	4,380	14	11
ALLEN MTN.	4,345	16.2	13
ESTHER MTN.	4,270	9.4	8
BIG SLIDE MTN.	4,255	9.4	7.5
STREET MTN.	4,216	12.7	11
UPPER WOLFJAW	4,203	8.7	8
LOWER WOLFJAW	4,173	8.8	9.5
PHELPS MTN.	4,160	10	9
SAWTEETH	4,138	11.8	9
SEYMOUR MTN.	4,120	14	11
MT. DONALDSON	4,108	17	17
CASCADE MTN.	4,098	4.8	5
MT. COLVIN	4,074	10.8	10
PORTER MTN.	4,070	7.6	5.5
SOUTH DIX	4,060	11.5	12
MT. EMMONS	4,039	18	18
EAST DIX	4,012	12.5	12
DIAL MTN.	4,003	10	9
BLAKE	3,960	13.6	12
CLIFF MTN.	3,944	17.2	12
NYE MTN.	3,888	7.5	8.5
COUCHSACHRAGA PEAK	3,793	15	12

For those of you counting, that's 578.4 miles round-trip, 490 hours of hiking, and 202,813 feet of combined elevation, 7 times the elevation of Mount Everest.

THE THOUSANDTH MAN

BY RUDYARD KIPLING

One man in a thousand, Solomon says,
Will stick more close than a brother.
And it's worth while seeking him half your days
If you find him before the other.

Nine hundred and ninety-nine depend
On what the world sees in you,
But the Thousandth Man will stand your friend
With the whole round world agin you.

'Tis neither promise nor prayer nor show
Will settle the finding for 'ee.
Nine hundred and ninety-nine of 'em go
By your looks, or your acts, or your glory.

But if he finds you and you find him
The rest of the world don't matter;
For the Thousandth Man will sink or swim
With you in any water.

You can use his purse with no more talk
Than he uses yours for his spendings,
And laugh and meet in your daily walk
As though there had been no lendings.

Nine hundred and ninety-nine of 'em call
For silver and gold in their dealings;
But the Thousandth Man he's worth 'em all
Because you can show him your feelings.

His wrong's your wrong, and his right's your right,
In season or out of season.
Stand up and back it in all men's sight
With that for your only reason!

Nine hundred and ninety-nine can't bide
The shame or mocking or laughter,
But the Thousandth Man will stand by your side
To the gallows-foot—and after!

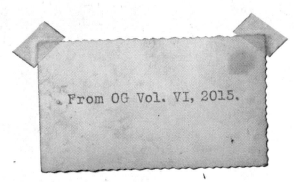

There is no surer way of making yourself popular on a camping trip, or for that matter in a household, than knowing how to cook. We have a battered old family recipe book which keeps us going at home during the summers, and if we ever hike out into the woods. It was first put together in the early 1950s by Charles Watson Whistler, his wife, Meg, and their four children. The kids got to put their favorite recipe on the cover, the ice-and-milk banana shake. Their blender conked out in 1978, according to Dad, but the family splurged on a replacement soon after—in 1993.

« BANANA SHAKE »

---

2 or 3 bananas, broken into pieces
2 cups of ice cubes or crushed ice
1 cup of milk

Place banana, ice, and a little of the milk in a blender. Blend slowly to start with to break down the ice cubes. Once they're broken into smaller pieces, increase the speed. Stop if it sounds like something is stuck and remove the object—ice or banana—using a long spoon. Once the mixture is smooth and you're blending quickly, pour in the rest of the milk and blend for another 20 seconds or so at top speed. Taste, add sugar if necessary, and pour into tall, preferably cold glasses.

« FLAPJACKS (PANCAKES) »

---

1 cup of flour
2 tablespoons of sugar
2 teaspoons of baking powder
A dash of salt
1 cup of milk
1 egg, beaten and added to the milk
And if you can be bothered, a couple of tablespoons of melted butter

---

- Mix the dry ingredients.

- Mix the wet ingredients.

- Then mix them all together until smooth.

- Heat a flat-bottomed pan.

- Dollop the pancake mix onto the pan, a couple of tablespoons at a time, into circles the size of a tennis ball. When bubbles start to appear on the surface, flip them. About a minute later, remove and slather with whatever you like: syrup, jam, butter, or nothing at all.

- If you're out in the wild, you can also just mix up flour and water till you have a thickish paste and fry that up. Won't be so delicious, but it'll keep you going awhile.

« VEGETABLE SOUP »

ENOUGH FOR 6 CUPS

Whatever vegetables you have
Salt
Grits
Cheese
Butter

🌿 Fill a saucepan with 5 cups of water and bring it to a boil.

🌿 While the water is heating up, raid the refrigerator for vegetables like carrots, onions, mushrooms, zucchini, potatoes, etc. Shred them using the big holes on a box grater or a chopping knife until you have a large bowlful.

🌿 Take 3 large handfuls of salad greens and tear them into pieces about half the size of the palm of your hand. Add all of this to the boiling water with a pinch of salt. It will seem like you're stuffing the saucepan too full, but the greens will reduce dramatically when cooked.

🌿 Cook uncovered for 3 minutes. Add 3 tablespoons of grits to thicken it up. Turn the heat to low and leave it to cook for another 3 minutes.

🌿 Meanwhile grate some cheese, enough to sprinkle all over the soup.

🌿 Remove the soup from the boil, spoon it into bowls. Add a small piece of butter, no larger than a postage stamp, to the top of each bowl, then add the cheese.

🌿 Serve up to hungry and grateful family and friends.

« HAMBURGERS »

MAKES 4 QUARTER POUNDERS

1 pound of beef
Salt and pepper
Fixins

⏚ Take 1 pound of beef, freshly ground by a butcher, and slap it into a bowl.

⏚ Sprinkle half a tablespoon each of salt and pepper over the meat and mix in with your hands.

⏚ Take a quarter of the meat and mold a patty, half an inch to an inch thick. Make 3 more patties.

⏚ Heat up a grill or frying pan to sizzling hot. Slide your patties into the pan or onto the grill. Cook 4 to 5 minutes on each side.

⏚ Wash your hands, the bowl, and any other surfaces touched by the raw meat. Use hot water and soap.

⏚ Remove patties and place either straight on a plate or on a toasted sesame seed bun, with onions, lettuce, tomatoes, and ketchup as you please.

« BROWNIES »

---

2 ounces (2 squares) unsweetened chocolate
½ cup (1 stick) butter chopped into dice
1 cup sugar
2 large eggs, lightly beaten
½ teaspoon vanilla extract
¼ cup all-purpose flour
A pinch of salt
1 cup coarsely chopped walnuts

🍳 Preheat the oven to 325 degrees Fahrenheit.

🍳 Take an 8-inch square baking pan and smear it with butter and a dusting of flour.

🍳 Melt the chocolate, butter, and sugar in a saucepan over low heat.

🍳 Remove from heat then stir in the lightly beaten eggs, and the vanilla extract. Mix till smooth. Add the flour, the pinch of salt, and the walnuts, and mix again. Then pour the whole lot into the pan and pop it into the heated oven. Bake for around 40 minutes or until a fork poked into the center comes out clean.

« CHOCOLATE SANDWICH (BASICALLY A GRILLED CHEESE BUT WITH CHOCOLATE INSTEAD OF CHEESE) »

---

2 slices of good bread, sourdough if you can get it.
Butter
2 large squares of chocolate

✒ Butter the bread, then place the chocolate between the unbuttered sides. Heat a skillet over medium, then place the sandwich in the middle, weighed down by a plate or bowl. Leave it for 3 minutes or so before turning it over. When both sides are brown, it's time to eat. Prepare to get messy.

« BOILING EGGS »

✒ First, bring a small saucepan of water to a rolling boil—this means that it is really boiling, not just hot with tiny streams of bubbles coming to the surface. Then gently lower your eggs into the water. Soft-boiled eggs will take 6 minutes. Hard-boiled eggs will take 10 to 12 minutes plus a further 6 to 7 minutes in cold water to stop the cooking.

« WHALE STEAK »

In *Moby-Dick*, Captain Ahab gives the following instructions for cooking a whale steak:

"When you cook another whale steak for my private table here, I'll tell you what to do so as not to spoil it by overdoing. I hold the steak in one hand and show a live coal to it with the other; that done, dish it; d'ye hear?"

When ordering beef or lamb in a restaurant, people who want their meat only lightly cooked ask for it "rare." Those who want it hardly cooked at all ask for it "blue," the natural color of veins.

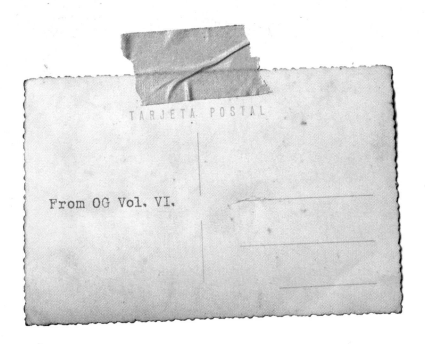

From OG Vol. VI.

August 2015

After a good feed, it's time to throw a ball around. Certain Whistlers are real bullies about this. Barely have we cleared the plates than they're reaching for the pigskin or a baseball mitt and hustling us all outside. My Dad can beg to be left alone to digest, but it's no use. It took me a while to learn to throw a football properly. The ball used to just fly out of my hand and flop around in the air, like an eggplant. I always wanted to throw those tight, fast spirals I saw NFL quarterbacks throw, the ones which zing through the freezing air of Lambeau Field or Giants Stadium, over the heads of defenders, towards a receiver who comes flying in from nowhere and races in for a touchdown. Finally, a friend of my Dad's who had played college football came up to Raquette Lake one weekend and showed me how. We found a clearing in the woods, and here's what he showed me.

First grip the ball with your fingers around the laces. If you have really big hands, like an NFL quarterback, your pinkie will touch the end of the ball. If you have normal-size hands, don't worry.

Hold it with both hands just below your chin.

Cock your throwing arm so the ball's around level with your ear and then use your other arm to point where you want the ball to go. If you want to throw a short, sharp pass, keep your shoulders level and snap your arm forward, pushing through your shoulders and hips. If you want to throw a long one, dip the shoulder of your throwing arm before you throw, so the ball goes higher.

Release the ball when your arm's slightly above your head. Flick your fingers and wrist as you throw to get spin and speed. You should feel the laces rotating off your fingers to get the spiral. You should end the throw with all your weight forward and your throwing hand pointing down to the ground.

It took a few afternoons of practice, but soon enough I had that ball leaving my hand like a bullet.

As for baseball, the best I can say is I do love a stadium hot dog. Back in 1948, as Major League Baseball was getting going again after World War Two, Charles Watson Whistler took his sons to Ebbets Field, the home of the Brooklyn Dodgers, and wrote and illustrated this short guide to pitching and baseball lingo. He included a poem about base stealing which came out that year.

July 1948

While there's nothing more fun than tossing a ball back and forth with a friend, to pitch a baseball well, you need to start with a couple of basic pitches: one hard and fast; one soft to confuse the batter. There are lots more that you can learn—the slider, the knuckleball, the forkball—but if you have these two, you'll at least be useful on the mound. The fastball's the classic, the essential pitch. The change-up, done right, should leave the batter flailing around, confused, like he dropped his keys and his pants fell down at the same time.

The basic fastball, the four-seam fastball, is the most dependable pitch in baseball. Curve your index and second fingers around the horseshoe seam and press your third and pinkie fingers down towards your palm. Your thumb will hold the underside of the ball, pressed against the smooth leather within the lower horseshoe. You should grip the ball softly, leaving a gap between it and your palm, so that when you throw it you spin it out of your hand with the most backspin and speed you can manage. It should reach the batter hard and fast without falling.

The three-finger change-up is ideal if you don't have very big hands. You curve your three middle fingers over the top of the horseshoe seam and tuck your thumb and pinkie finger beneath the ball, touching them together. Then tuck the ball deep into your palm. This will take some speed off the ball when you throw it with the same arm speed as you would a fastball. The change in speed should trick the batter.

Baseball has a language all to itself. Up in the stands, you'll hear many of these terms, and given the salty tongues of our Brooklyn friends, doubtless many less printable.

✎ ACE Your best starting pitcher.

✎ ALLEYS The areas of the outfield between the outfielders.

✎ BACKDOOR SLIDER A pitch that appears to be out of the strike zone but then breaks back over the plate.

✎ BALTIMORE CHOP A ground ball that hits in front of home plate (or off of it) and takes a large hop over the infielder's head.

✎ BANDBOX A small, hitter-friendly ballpark, like Boston's Fenway Park.

✎ BANG-BANG PLAY When the base runner hits the bag a split second before the ball arrives or vice versa.

✎ BRONX CHEER When the crowd boos, typically the friendly mob at Yankee Stadium.

✎ BRUSHBACK A pitch that nearly hits a batter.

✎ BUSH, OR BUSH LEAGUE An amateur play or behavior.

✎ CAN OF CORN An easy catch.

✐ CAUGHT LOOKING When a batter is called out on strikes.

✐ CHEESE A good fastball.

✐ CHIN MUSIC A pitch that flies high and inside around the batter's chin.

✐ DINGER A home run.

✐ FIREMAN A team's closer or late-inning relief pitcher.

✐ FUNGO A ball hit to a fielder during practice with a "fungo bat," longer and thinner than a regular bat.

✐ GOPHER BALL A pitch hit for a home run, as in "go for."

✐ HEAT, OR HEATER A good fastball.

✐ HIGH AND TIGHT A pitch up in the strike zone and inside on a hitter; also known as "up and in."

✐ HOMER A home run, moon shot, blast, dinger, dong, four-bagger, four-base knock, and tater.

✐ JAMMED When the pitch sails close to the hitter's hands.

✐ LEATHER As in "flashing the leather" of your glove; making a good defensive play.

✐ MEATBALL An easy pitch to hit.

✐ ON THE SCREWS When a batter hits the ball hard; also "on the button."

✐ PAINTING THE BLACK When a pitcher throws over the edge of the plate.

✐ PICK A good defensive play by an infielder on a ground ball; short for "pick-off."

✐ PICKLE A rundown.

✐ RHUBARB A fight or scuffle.

✐ RIBBIE Another way of saying RBI; also known as a "ribeye."

✐ RUBBER GAME The deciding game of a series.

✐ RUNDOWN When a base runner gets caught between bases by the fielders.

✐ RUTHIAN Powerfully, like Babe Ruth, the Yankee slugger.

✐ SOUTHPAW A left-handed pitcher.

✆ SWEET SPOT The part of the bat just a few inches up the barrel which hits the ball best.

✆ TEXAS LEAGUER A bloop hit that drops between an infielder and outfielder.

✆ TOOLS OF IGNORANCE A catcher's equipment.

✆ UNCLE CHARLIE A curveball.

✆ WHEELHOUSE A hitter's power zone, waist-high and over the heart of the plate.

✆ WHEELS A player's legs.

✆ WHIFF A strikeout.

✆ YAKKER A curveball.

THE BASE STEALER

BY ROBERT FRANCIS

Poised between going on and back, pulled
Both ways taut like a tightrope-walker,
Fingertips pointing the opposites,
Now bouncing tiptoe like a dropped ball
Or a kid skipping rope, come on, come on,
Running a scattering of steps sidewise,
How he teeters, skitters, tingles, teases,
Taunts them, hovers like an ecstatic bird,
He's only flirting, crowd him, crowd him,
Delicate, delicate, delicate, delicate—now!

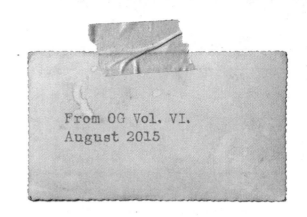

From OG Vol. VI.
August 2015

About a week ago, I took part in a sailing race on the lake and blew it. I was in the lead at the final turn and starting to think about winning. I lost my focus and tacked when I shouldn't have. I was furious with myself and cursed my bad luck to Dad. He didn't say much, but just put his arm round me and walked me home. A couple of days later, I woke up to find a letter tucked under my door.

CW

Dear Charlie,

After you were beaten at the line the other day, you blamed your luck. I've been noodling on this and thought you might like to think on it.

In 1911, two teams raced to be the first to reach the South Pole. Robert Falcon Scott, an Englishman, led one team; Roald Amundsen, a Norwegian, the other.

They set about their task in different ways. For Scott, the journey was also about science and conducting experiments in the undiscovered wilderness of Antarctica. Amundsen had just one goal: getting to the Pole as quickly as possible and returning home safely.

127

"Lucky Amundsen"

"Not So Lucky Scott"

For Amundsen, every decision he made in planning his expedition had to serve his single goal. He began by mapping out the shortest possible route, which began at a point on the Great Ice Barrier where no previous explorer had camped. This meant he started sixty miles closer to the Pole than previous expeditions which had set out from McMurdo Sound. Scott played it safe. He followed precedent and began at McMurdo Sound, meaning he had 120 miles farther to travel round-trip than his rival.

Amundsen then considered transport. He and Scott had bought the same wooden sleds. But Amundsen's team shaved off two-thirds of the sleds' weight to make them easier to move. Every pound of weight would matter on their freezing, energy-sapping journey.

Amundsen's team was stripped-down and lean: five men and a team of dogs. Every man could make, mend, and improve his own equipment if need be. Amundsen chose dogs to pull the sleds because they were quick, strong, and indifferent to the cold. They took care of themselves at night by burrowing into holes in the snow to keep warm. They could eat pretty much anything—even

Scott's dog Chris listening to the gramophone.
If your job was to get to the South Pole,
would you bring a gramophone?

each other if it came to that. And they were fun to be around on those long slogs across the snow.

Scott brought 16 men, 23 dogs, 10 ponies, 13 sledges, and 2 motor sledges, a real circus. The ponies were good haulers, but they could not tolerate the snow. Their sweat would turn to ice on their hides and weigh them down. Every night, Scott's men had to build walls of snow around the ponies to keep them warm. It was exhausting for everyone and eventually the ponies had to be put down.

The motor sledges kept breaking down and had to be abandoned. And then halfway to the Pole, Scott sent back his dogs as he didn't think they could cross all the crevasses he imagined lay in his path. So his men had to haul their heavy sleds themselves. Scott thought there was something noble about men hauling their own luggage—though it seems like madness to me.

Amundsen fussed over every detail. He designed the trunks carrying his supplies and equipment so he could open and close them without having to unstrap them from their sleds. Scott's team, on the other hand, had to load and unload their trunks from their sleds every day just to get at their things.

When it came to food, both men knew the importance of leaving well-marked stores as they advanced to the Pole, so they could eat them on their way back. But Amundsen was extra-cautious. He brought 10 times the food Scott did. And he marked each stash of food with black flags running five miles to the left and right, so if he lost his way in a blizzard he might still have a chance of finding them. Scott marked his stashes with just one flag.

Amundsen's men actually gained weight on their way back from the Pole. Scott's team died of starvation.

Amundsen reached the Pole and planted the Norwegian flag 35 days before Scott got there.

There was nobility in Scott's failure, I suppose. His team showed astounding courage. On their return journey, his men died one by one. One of them, Captain Lawrence Oates, suffered from terrible frostbite and scurvy. Rather than slowing down his companions, he walked out of his tent one morning into a howling blizzard, knowing he would die. Scott wrote in his diary: "We knew that poor Oates was walking to his death, but though we tried to dissuade him, we knew it was the act of a brave man and an English gentleman."

All mighty fine stuff. But was it really necessary? When he returned from Antarctica, Amundsen was asked what separated triumph from disaster: "I may say that this is the greatest factor—the way in which the expedition is equipped—the way in which every difficulty is foreseen, and precautions taken for meeting or avoiding it. Victory awaits him who has everything in order—luck, people call it. Defeat is certain for him who has neglected to take the necessary precautions in time; this is called bad luck." Scott blamed his failure on "misfortune."

Perhaps you were unlucky in that race. Or perhaps you were simply underprepared. In every race you'll ever run, there'll be an Amundsen and a Scott, one fully prepared and victorious, the other underprepared and all too ready to blame bad luck.

Yours (lucky for you),
Dad

(P.S. All of this talk of luck reminds me that I'd never found it easy to explain the term "irony" till someone put it like this: irony's when you've got a dog called Lucky and it gets run over by a car.)

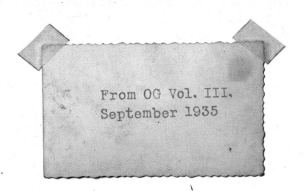

From OG Vol. III.
September 1935

THE RAQUETTE REPORTER

The Leaping Lizard Returns to Lake George

BY CHARLIE WHISTLER

There is nothing special about George Reis's boathouse on Lake George. It is much like every other. Wooden, damp, creaky, with a concrete ramp going down into the water. But inside lives a legend: *El Lagarto*, "The

Leaping Lizard," three-time winner of the Gold Cup, the greatest prize in powerboat racing.

She is a slender craft, 25 feet and 10 inches long, 5 foot 6 inches across at her widest point, enough room for two drivers to sit side by side, provided they don't mind an elbow in their ribs.

Ignore that the mahogany on her deck doesn't match. The real action is down below, on her stepped hull, which skips across the water like a flat stone, faster than any rival. She may be 13 years old, geriatric in boat years, but she's still quick. "Faster than fire in a flaming cane break," one admiring sea dog called her, "and quicker than a frightened rabbit."

Two years ago, she slipped into the Gold Cup race unnoticed. The cupholder that year was Horace Elgin Dodge Jr., heir to the Dodge automotive fortune. He was hosting the race on the Detroit River, in the heart of his home city. The Detroit swells had gathered on the riverbanks to bet on which of Dodge's four entrants in the big race would carry off the trophy. None fancied *El Lagarto*, piloted by Reis and his friend Dick Bowers, both summer residents of Lake George.

But as the seven boats in the race came roaring towards the starting line, and the starting gun fired, it was *El Lagarto* who flashed into an early lead. None of Dodge's high-class speedsters could catch her as she loped, or "porpoised," across the water, like a dolphin. She had the speed of a Thoroughbred and the strength of a dray. She whipped the field and silenced the sneering fans of Motor City who had called her "pretty near old enough to marry Mahatma Gandhi."

Last year, she won again, this time on her home waters of Lake George, beating the fastest boats in the world over 90 heart-pounding miles of racing.

This year, confidence again was high. Reis is a poet and actor by trade and loves to gather children round the boathouse, while Smoke Gates, his mechanic, clangs away inside and Bowers sips a beer on the wharf. We just park our bikes and listen.

The reason he'd got into racing in the first place, he told us, was to beat his neighbor on the lake, a New York City businessman called Jonathan Moore. Moore was unbeaten on Lake George in his boat *Jolly Roger* and too smug about it for Reis's liking. So in 1925, Reis went out and bought himself the stout *Miss Mary*, which he renamed *El Lagarto*,

"The Lizard." He took the name from his brother's home in Palm Springs, California, which swarms with the reptiles.

Reis promptly beat Moore. Moore tried to up the stakes with a new boat called *Falcon*, but still couldn't cut it and eventually gave up. But Reis now had a taste for racing.

The big question in speedboat racing, he explained, waving away a swarm of bugs, is: how fast can you go without losing control? Anyone can go faster. Just strap on a bigger engine. But you still have to be able to steer your boat and handle big waves. In 1933, *El Lagarto* continued to do this better than anyone. He said that *El Lagarto* ran so smoothly at high speed, he could take his hands clean off the wheel in midrace.

Such confidence, though, nearly proved disastrous. Five days before this year's Gold Cup, Reis and Bowers took her out for a spin and her engine clattered to a stop. They dismantled it and rushed it to the factory where it had been built.

Two days straight, nights too, the mechanics worked till finally *El Lagarto*'s engine came back to life. With just hours to go, Smoke Gates raced to fit the engine back onto the boat. She was ready. Just.

As she bounded up towards the starting line, the crowds on the shore cheered. Dodge and his boats were yet again no match. *El Lagarto* porpoised away into the distance, and triumphed for the third year in a row.

Viva El Lagarto!

From OG Vol. IV. Eleanor was the daughter
of Charles Wetherby Whistler and the
sister of Charles Watson Whistler. She was
a member of the Adirondack 46ers and a
doctor in New York. People would gather
along the banks of the Adirondack lakes to
watch her cast a fishing rod, and land her
fly right in the mouth of a giant trout.
Whenever my grandfather, to whom she wrote
this letter, spoke about her, he'd shake his
head, smile, and say the same thing: "Boy,
was she a pistol."

September 1948

ELEANOR WHISTLER

Dear Charlie,

It is late September already, and fall has yet to come to the city. Just walking from home to work is like taking a steam bath. During meetings my mind keeps drifting back to the lake. The sound of the waves lapping up below the boathouse. The zip, splash, Holy Toledo!!! as we jump into the bracing, green water, so cold it makes my teeth ache. I could use a swim about now. Though without you trying to dunk me—for once.

Your father tells me that he's spoken to his friends in the Mohawk tribe. The date for your hunt is set for late October. It's one of the weekends when you're home. I realize it must seem rather strange for

us to be sending you out with the Mohawk when we have our own ways and traditions of hunting. But it was something I did at your age, and the experience has never left me. Not just the hunting, but the whole ritual, before and after. So much of our lives is devoted to conquering nature, to fending it off with walls and roofs. To channeling it with dams and roads and tunnels. To killing it for pure sport.

But there is another way of living and it's worth experiencing at least once. It's never a bad idea to take the way you live and think and give it a good shake from time to time. The way we live is always changing, as it is for the Mohawk.

I was 12, like you, when I first went out with the Mohawk. It was unusual for a girl to go out, but your grandfather thought it important. It was late fall, the start of the hunting season. The deer were charging through the woods, which meant we were in for a deep winter.

We humans rely on weather forecasts, but the animals sense the coming weather in a quite different way. The squirrels and bears hoard, the birds migrate, and the deer get ready by fattening up and gathering in groups to prepare their beds, sheltered from the wind. They were working unusually early that year.

My father woke me on a Friday morning. The woodstove was lit, the pancakes were made. As I swung out of bed and put my feet on the floor, I pulled them up again quickly. Summer had long gone. The floorboards were freezing. In the kitchen, Father was standing at the window drinking coffee. The sun was rising slowly. Reluctantly. Like you on a Sunday morning. I ate the pancakes, covered in what was left of the spring's maple syrup. As I slurped up the last of them, I saw a man leading a boy and a girl up to the house. Father opened the door before they could knock.

They wore deerskin leggings and embroidered shirts. Their ink black hair was cut short. Father waved me over.

"Ellie. Let me introduce you to my friends. Falling Rain," the girl nodded. "Blazing Arrow," the boy nodded. "And their father. Peter."

"My tribe calls me Running Water," said Peter. "But I have been working so long as a hunting guide to others that it has been easier to have a name like yours."

"I like Running Water just fine," I said. Father put his hand on my shoulder.

"Call him whatever he lets you. And do whatever he says. There is no finer guide in the Adirondacks. I will see you tomorrow afternoon." He handed me my knife in its leather sheath. "Everything else you need, Peter will help."

I remember setting off that day feeling nervous, venturing out into those woods without my own family for once. In the company of strangers, albeit friendly ones. We spent the first hour walking in silence. No pleasantries or idle chitchat. No asking me how I liked school or what my favorite subject was. Just crunching deeper and deeper into the woods.

"Look," said Running Water, stopping for the first time. He bent down and pointed to hoof nicks on a log. "The deer come through here." It wasn't obvious, but when I looked I could see the faint outline of a path, where the scrubby plants had been kicked down. There were traces of scat. The two Mohawk children were cupping their ears forward using their thumb and index fingers. I did the same. Suddenly, the sounds of the forest became clearer. I could make out the pecking of a woodpecker, the distant cackle of loons, and the flute of a wood thrush. Running Water bent the slender branch of a low bush to show me where the deer had bitten off the leaves.

"Do you know the weasel walk?" Falling Rain asked me. She squatted low to the ground, then began moving, setting each foot down slowly, the outer ball of the foot first, then the inner ball, then the arch and the heel. "You feel the ground under you. And you don't snap the twigs. Your press them down." The first time I tried, I toppled over onto my rear. The kids laughed. But I brushed myself down and tried again. "Everything must be slow. And flowing," said Falling Rain, who squatted down beside me. "If you feel an animal looking at you, you must freeze, completely still. No noise." We went round in circles for a while doing the weasel walk until we'd stopped laughing and Falling Rain was sure I had the hang of it.

Peter raised his finger to his lips and gestured for us all to crouch down. I could not see a thing. And after a few moments, Peter waved us up again.

"A big buck. A hundred yards away. Did you see it?" The Mohawk kids nodded.

"Don't try to focus," said Blazing Arrow. "Relax your eyes so you can take in everything in front of you." Each individual object was blurred, but I could now sense movement and shapes across a much wider area. I could see a small bush move far off to my right as a rabbit darted out. I could sense the slightest movement of the trees.

"Now, you need some camouflage," said Peter. He picked up a handful of dirt and rubbed it into my hair. "This will take the shine off. And some of the soap. You're too clean for this work. The animals will smell you." He took a piece of charcoal from his pocket and rubbed it on my cheeks and forehead.

We kept walking. It had rained the day before, and we could make out tracks in the mud. The dainty trot of the deer, following their familiar and predictable paths through the forest. The swift, purposeful gait of the coyote and gray wolf. I could imagine them darting along, not wasting an ounce of energy, alert to every opportunity and danger.

"We try to become like them," said Falling Rain, who was walking along beside me. "Before the hunt, we go into a hot room to sweat out our human smells and empty our minds of anything which could distract us. During the hunt, you can't be thinking of anything else. The animals will pick up on your distraction and run."

The woods became darker and deeper, the paths less obvious. I could just about glimpse the sun passing over us at midday. We came to a large rock, which reared out of the forest floor, like the hump of a whale. We pressed up against it. I relaxed my eyes. Far off to our left, I saw a young buck walking slowly towards us. He was sniffing the ground, then the air, then the ground again. He sensed something, but not enough to scare him. He kept walking. I stopped breathing and stood as still as I could, frightened I would snap a twig and send the buck running. Falling Rain and Blazing Arrow stood on either side of me, their bows at the ready. I could hear the buck now, its hooves softly striking the earth, the rustle of branches as it chewed off what buds and leaves were left.

And then it was there. Twenty feet away. It was a difficult shot. The arrow would have to thread through the trees. Falling Rain was ready to fire, her string drawn. But she waited. The deer sniffed at something on the ground, then raised its head towards us. I could swear it looked straight at me. It knew something was there, but now seemed scared to move. Falling Rain fired. Her arrow sang from her bow and struck the deer right in the heart. It staggered, then fell to its knees, groaning in pain.

Peter ran towards it, jumping over fallen logs. He stood a few feet back. The buck raised its head one last time, then fell back down. Peter knelt over it, as if in prayer. We ran to join him. Blazing Arrow unsheathed his knife and was about to begin work field-dressing the buck, when he stopped and turned the knife's handle over to me. I must have looked panicked because Blazing Arrow smiled reassuringly and said: "It is as much a part of hunting as the killing."

He showed me the point just below the deer's neck where I was to cut. The knife went in easily. Blazing Arrow told me to pull upwards, away from the deer's innards. My stomach growled unhappily as I dug in and pulled. The hide tore like an old canvas sail. I could feel the warmth of the deer's guts and blood on my cold hands. I remember wincing, not wanting to carry on. I was frightened I would vomit and embarrass myself. But my three guides watched patiently. Once I had cut the deer open as far as I could, Falling Rain cut open the rest. She then reached inside with her hand, and told me to do the same. Together we pulled out the stomach. She reached in farther with her knife to cut out the heart and lungs, which slithered out onto my knees. Blazing Arrow and Peter then pushed the buck onto its stomach so that the rest of its innards could fall out onto the ground.

Peter gathered up the heart and liver and put them into a small bag which hung at his waist.

"We were lucky," he said. "We're just a mile from home." He cut down a thick branch and set about tying up the buck by its legs. Peter then took the rear and Blazing Arrow and I the front. Even without its insides, the deer weighed heavily on our shoulders. Falling Rain walked ahead, clearing the way, pointing out hidden stumps and branches. It must have taken us an hour to reach camp.

There were three longhouses and a couple of smaller buildings in a clearing surrounded by a fence. I had seen pictures of such camps in books, but nothing quite prepared me for the real thing. The longhouses were made of bent saplings, covered in wide layers of bark. In between were scaffolds, hung with animal carcasses and skins. Everything here served a particular purpose. Nothing was wasted. The men and women seemed to move more slowly than people in the world I was used to, drifting from place to place in clouds of wood smoke.

We hung up our buck to drain and cool down. Peter cut a few strips of fresh meat and then led us back out of the camp. We walked a good distance before Peter stopped beside a fallen tree, which had been propped up on two cut logs. He laid the meat between the logs.

"The bear will try to eat the meat, and knock over the logs," Falling Rain explained. The tree would then fall and kill it. She said it so matter-of-factly. As if killing a black bear was no stranger than going to buy groceries. Which, of course, for her, it wasn't. It was not cruel, nor savage, nor sporting. It was simply the way of things. You killed animals, but did so respectfully, using all they gave you, their skins as clothing, their bones as tools, and their flesh as food. You never wasted the gift of their lives.

That night I slept in a longhouse, on skins laid out on the floor, staring up at strings of apples and herbs hung from the ceiling. Tucked in a corner were masks for the False Face Society. Twice a year, in spring and fall, members of the tribe put on these masks and dance through the village shaking rattles to drive away sickness. The faces on the masks were hideously distorted. The mouths were askew, the noses bulbous and crooked. Their cheeks were smeared with tobacco and sunflower oil stains, where they had been "fed." The moonlight slanted through

144

a square hole in the roof. Blazing Arrow and Falling Rain lay on either side of me. Falling Rain pointed up to one of the masks and said with a giggle: "That one is Long Nose, the kidnapper of naughty children."

As the fire burned down in the center of the room, Peter told us a story. It came to him from travelers to the tribes who live along the Pacific coast.

Late one summer, a group of girls set out to pick berries. As they reached the woods, they began to sing to warn the bears that they were coming. All except one, the chief's daughter. She refused. "The bears don't deserve my singing," she said, haughtily.

By late afternoon, the girls had filled their baskets and it was time to return home. As they walked back, the chief's daughter's basket handle broke. She scampered to pick up the fruit which fell all over the path, while the other girls walked on ahead. Once she had refilled her basket, she set off again. But before she could catch up, the handle broke again. Once again, she picked up the fruit and mended the handle. But as she sat beside the path, the light faded. She could no longer hear her friends.

She heard a twig snap behind her and whirled around. A young man in a bearskin cloak was walking towards her. "Give me your basket," he said. "It's too late for you to return home. You will come and stay with us."

She followed him to his village, into the largest house of all. Peering through the smoky darkness, she saw people sitting on benches around the walls, each wrapped in a bearskin. An old man with a crown of bear claws sat on a higher seat than the others.

"She is beautiful," said the old man. "A worthy wife for you, my nephew." He then spoke to the girl. "Please eat with us. Your new husband, my nephew, will sit beside you."

The girl sat down. She began to cry. An old woman stepped beside her and whispered in her ear. "You insulted the bears this morning by refusing to sing. Now do what you are told. If you try to run away, they will kill you."

From that day on, the girl learned the ways of the Bear People. She watched as they turned into bears the moment they left the village to hunt. Her husband was kind to her but she cried whenever she remembered her parents and brothers.

Her villagers sent out search parties to find her, but with no success. Her brothers were convinced she was alive, and that the bears had taken her. Day after day, they set out with their dog, killing any bears they met.

One day, the Bear Chief's nephew took his wife by the hand and said: "We must leave. Your brothers will soon reach the village. I will take you far up the mountain where they will never find you."

They climbed for days through the snow, until they came to a cave, where they could survive the winter. And here, the girl bore twins, half human, half bear.

One day, while her husband slept, the girl heard voices. She looked down from the cave and saw her four brothers and their dog. She waved and shouted, but the wind carried away her cries. She threw a snowball which arced through the air and landed at the feet of her youngest brother. He peered up the mountain, but saw nothing. The dog sniffed the snowball and began to bark. He could smell where the girl had touched it. The brothers now saw their sister waving.

Her husband woke up. "I dreamed this would happen," he said, mournfully. "That one day your brothers would kill me. But I shan't fight them. Just ask them to treat me with respect. Not to drag my body

147

along the ground. And once I am skinned, to hang me with my head facing the sun." He left the cave to face his death.

The girl and her brothers hugged, happy to be reunited.

When she returned to her village, the girl was welcomed with a great feast. For a while, she was delighted to be home. But the longer she stayed, the more she thought back to the Bear People. Her appearance had changed during her time away. Soft brown fur had begun to grow up her legs and arms and down her back. She moved out of her family's home to a smaller home on the edge of the village, where she could be alone with her bear-children.

One day as winter approached, her youngest brother brought her some bearskins with which to make clothing. As she felt the fur, she could not resist wrapping herself up in it, and wrapping it around her two children.

She took one last look at her village. This was no longer her home. She led her cubs up into the mountains and they were never seen again.

That story haunted me all night in the longhouse, and I think of it still today. How different are we really from bears, deer, and any other creature?

The next morning, after breakfast, we returned to the bear trap. A black bear had poked its head in to take the meat and been crushed by a falling log.

Falling Rain could see I was upset. She took my hand.

"Don't worry. We shall do what is right with him."

I returned to our cabin with my clothes, my hair, everything smelling of wood smoke. Father was waiting outside for me, smoking his pipe.

"How was she?" he said.

"A fine student," said Peter.

I waved good-bye to my three guides and watched them walk back into the woods. As they left, I realized that it wasn't their world that seemed strange anymore. It was the one I was returning to.

You'll have your own experience, of course, Charlie. Well, I hope you do. There's no point reliving the same old thing. But mine never left me, and I hope yours doesn't either.

Visit me soon. Some aunts are all lace and bonbons. But not this one. I need my roustabout nephew to keep things lively.

With all my love—and good hunting!
Aunt Eleanor

August 1871 by Charles Wetherby Whistler

It's easy to forget how ancient these Adirondacks are. Long before our breathless arrival, they were someone else's home. Last night, a clergyman in Long Lake invited one of the Algonquin chiefs to talk to a group of us in a clearing in the woods. The chief was a large, handsome fellow with a soft voice. He told us that we might look at these forests and see a place of beauty and recreation. Others might see a chance to make money, by chopping down the trees. But to him and his tribe, stories and spirits drifted like wisps along every path, enveloping every wave, leaf, and rock.

Long before the Europeans arrived in North America, he told us, a forest spread from east to west, from what is now Maine to Minnesota. It was dotted with lakes, mountains, and curling rivers. In this forest lived the Algonquin, Iroquois, and other tribes. They crossed their land by water and along foot-worn tracks. They called these woods the Great Longhouse, their home.

But as in any home, people became jealous of each other. The tribe which lived in Indian Carry, that patch of land between Raquette River and Saranac Lake across which you have to carry your canoe, loathed the tribe which lived by Tupper Lake. If two members of these tribes ever met in the woods, rarely did both escape alive.

It was unfortunate, then, that Howling Wind, a young man from Indian Carry, fell in love with a young woman from Tupper Lake. It was even more unfortunate that she felt the same way. To conceal their affection, they communicated by secret messages and met in hidden places. But one moonlit evening, Howling Wind abandoned his usual caution. He decided to row out to a spot on Tupper Lake called Devil's Rock, which was always said to be cursed. There in the cold night, he told the young woman the story of the Rock. "The devil lashed together a raft and for an oar, he used his long, lizardy tail. He whipped that tail back and forth through the water, splish, splash, and came to this point. Then he summoned all the fish in the lake and the animals in the woods, saying he was going to preach to them." So vividly did Howling Wind tell the story that the poor girl shivered with fear. "But just as they had gathered round, the devil pounced! He gobbled them all up, every last one." "Enough!" said the girl. Howling Wolf laughed and put his arm around her. "It's just a story."

From far on the other side of the lake, a young man from Tupper Lake, called Red Cloud, was spying on them. He too loved the girl and was jealous of Howling Wind. He raced back to the camp and blurted out what he had seen. The other tribesmen gathered up their weapons, donned their war paint, and set out to exact revenge.

Racing through the woods, they soon caught up with Howling Wind and the girl. The moonlight fell like fine snow through the pine trees. Howling Wind raised his spear. But the tribesmen rushed him and wrestled him to the ground. He slashed at his attackers but they were too strong. They dragged him back to Tupper Lake for judgment.

After a short deliberation, the eldest of the elders announced the sentence. "Howling Wind must be killed. And the girl must kill him." She fell to her knees and begged. Such cruelty! If he had to be killed, let someone else do it! The elders ignored her. They placed an ax in her hands. Suddenly, she stopped crying. She gripped the ax tightly. The tribesmen watched in gleeful silence. Howling Wind was bound to a tree. He stared at her as she approached. She raised the tomahawk and with one blow, slashed through the ropes which held him. Then she turned to Red Cloud, who was running towards her, and brought the ax down on his skull, splitting it in two. The lovers ran, their hands entwined, their feet, quickened by fear, barely touching the pine-strewn ground, until they ran into a party from Indian Carry. They were on their way to rescue him. Together they all went home. Howling Wind and his bride lived a long, contented life.

From OG Vol. VI.

Summer 2015

Storms explode here on the lake. The air turns heavy. People jerk up their heads like deer when they hear a snap of a twig and fear a hunter may be near. They hurry to shelter. Anyone out on the lake paddles hard to shore hoping to outrun the weather. The Jet Skis roar in. The lake can be smooth as glass one minute, shattered the next by raindrops the size of golf balls. Dark clouds whoosh low across the water so fast you can hear them. Then the real rain comes, sloshing down in sheets. The electricity inside the house flickers. We sit in open doors and out on the porch, watching the last stragglers race in, holding sodden newspapers and ruined books above their heads. Then as quickly as it comes, the storm is gone, taking the muggy day with it. The air is fresh, and it's time to sprint down the dock and leap into the rain-warmed water of the lake.

This is when I like to grab my binoculars and notebook and go looking for birds. The Adirondacks seem to have as many kinds of birds as New York City has people. These are the ones I've seen, or still have on my "to-see" list: Wood Warbler, American Bittern, Kestrel, Saw-Whet Owl,

Northern Goshawk, Gray Jay, Boreal Chickadee, Black-Backed Woodpecker, Mourning Warblers, Bluebirds, Common Snipe, Gray Catbird, Red-Breasted Nuthatch, Common Loon, Spruce Grouse, Palm Warbler, Lincoln's Sparrow, Yellow-Bellied Flycatchers, Sharp-Shinned Hawk, Red-Shouldered Hawk, Eastern Wood Pewee, Common Raven, Brown Creeper, Winter Wren, Golden-Crowned Kinglet, Swainson's Warbler, Northern Parula, Chestnut-Sided Warbler, Magnolia Warbler, Black-Throated Blue Warbler, Yellow-Rumped Warbler, Pine Warbler, Black-and-White Warbler, American Redstart, Ovenbird, Scarlet Tanager, Swamp Sparrow, White-Throated Sparrow, Woodpeckers, Olive-Sided Flycatchers, Nashville Warbler, Great Blue Heron, Tree Swallow, Eastern Bluebirds, and the Great Horned Owl.

I write down the name of every bird I see and the place and time I see it. In my notebook, I follow the example of John James Audubon, who painted the *Birds of America*, and wrote vertically and horizontally to save paper.

Like many of the best people, Audubon didn't have things easy. He was born in 1785 and had a happy boyhood in Brittany, France, roaming the fields, gathering birds' eggs and nests, flowers, and pebbles. But then his father, Jean Audubon, who had fought in the American Revolution, decided his son needed to be "toughened up" and sent him to a farm he had bought in Pennsylvania called Mill Grove. Here Audubon lived with an American family and began drawing birds.

He decided to create a collection of drawings and paintings of American birds, which he hoped to sell. He wanted to depict the birds as they appeared in nature, so he killed them (with fine shot, so he didn't damage their feathers) and arranged them with wire into the precise poses he wanted. To support himself while he assembled his collection of paintings, he taught drawing, music, dancing, and fencing and even worked as a taxidermist. At the age of 35, he lost most of his money in a bad investment and was then robbed of the rest.

He found himself in New Orleans without a bean. He wrote in his notebook that "nothing but the astonishing desire I have of compleating my work keeps my spirits at par."

Luckily, that was enough. He finished his work. And he sold it. The risks he took paid off for him and for us. In 2000, a copy of *Birds of America* broke the world record price for a book, selling for $8.8 million. And the Audubon Society, one of the most important conservation groups in America, bears his name.

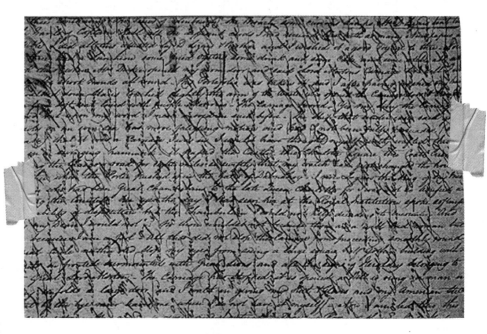

Audubon's notebook.

From OG Vol. VI, 2015.

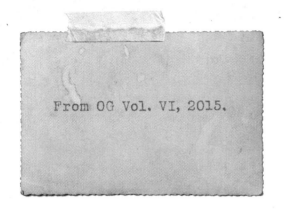

Three hundred years before Audubon, a Japanese calligrapher and artist called Jimyoin Motoharu created a series of books on falconry, the sport of hunting wild animals using a trained falcon. It was a sport for the rich and powerful in Japan and required sophisticated techniques, which were passed down through generations. Kind of like the advice in an Omnium Gatherum, handed down from Whistler to Whistler. What I liked about this drawing is the falcon's face. He doesn't seem too impressed to be the subject of all this study. I think he'd rather be left alone to do whatever it is falcons like to do.

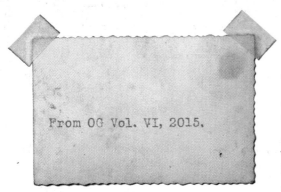

From OG Vol. VI, 2015.

Every so often, I'll see the bald eagle soaring high above the trees. One minute, it's just a fleck against the blue, next thing you know it's plummeting downwards. Just before it smacks into the lake, it slows down and grabs a fish which has made the mistake of coming up close to the surface. Then it's off into the woods with its lunch. That's the eagle at its best. Other times, it's a bully. It will see another hawk has caught a fish and lunge and dart around threateningly. When the hawk drops its catch, the eagle makes off with it. These gangster habits explain why Benjamin Franklin never wanted the eagle as our national symbol.

In 1784, two years after the eagle was chosen, he wrote to his daughter Sally that he'd have preferred the turkey. The bald eagle, he wrote, "is a Bird of bad moral Character. He does not get his Living honestly. You may have seen him perched on some dead Tree near the River, where, too lazy to fish for himself, he watches the Labour of the Fishing Hawk; and when that diligent Bird has at length taken a Fish, and is bearing it to his Nest for the Support of his Mate and young Ones, the Bald Eagle pursues him and takes it from him.

"With all this Injustice, he is never in good Case but like those among Men who live by Sharping & Robbing he is generally poor and often very lousy. Besides he is a rank Coward: The little King Bird not bigger than a Sparrow attacks him boldly and drives him out of the District. He

is therefore by no means a proper Emblem for the brave and honest Cincinnati of America who have driven all the King birds from our Country. . . .

"The Turkey is in Comparison a much more respectable Bird, and withal a true original Native of America. . . . He is besides, though a little vain & silly, a Bird of Courage, and would not hesitate to attack a Grenadier of the British Guards who should presume to invade his Farm Yard with a red Coat on."

Before he threw his support behind the turkey, though, Franklin's first choice was the rattlesnake. He once drew a cartoon of a Rattlesnake cut into pieces to encourage the various states to join forces against the French in the French and Indian War. New England is at the head, followed by the states in order as you move south down the East Coast of America, with South Carolina at the tail. In 1775, a year before the Declaration of Independence, he wrote a letter to the *Pennsylvania Journal* in which he proposed the rattlesnake as the symbol of a new and independent America. The rattlesnake was wise, lived a

159

long life, and was uniquely American. If you trod on it, the way the British had trod on the Americans, you risked painful retribution. He went on:

I recollected that her eye excelled in brightness, that of any other animal, and that she has no eye-lids. She may therefore be esteemed an emblem of vigilance. She never begins an attack, nor, when once engaged, ever surrenders: She is therefore an emblem of magnanimity and true courage. As if anxious to prevent all pretensions of quarreling with her, the weapons with which nature has furnished her, she conceals in the roof of her mouth, so that, to those who are unacquainted with her, she appears to be a most defenseless animal; and even when those weapons are shown and extended for her defense, they appear weak and contemptible; but their wounds however small, are decisive and fatal. Conscious of this, she never wounds 'till she has generously given notice, even to her enemy, and cautioned him against the danger of treading on her.

Was I wrong, Sir, in thinking this a strong picture of the temper and conduct of America? The poison of her teeth is the necessary means of digesting her food, and at the same time is certain destruction to her enemies. This may be understood to intimate that those things which are destructive to our enemies, may be to us not only harmless, but absolutely necessary to our existence. . . .

'Tis curious and amazing to observe how distinct and independent of each other the rattles of this animal are, and yet how firmly they are united together, so as never to be separated but by breaking them to pieces. One of those rattles singly, is incapable of producing sound, but the ringing of thirteen together, is sufficient to alarm the boldest man living.

The Rattle-Snake is solitary, and associates with her kind only when it is necessary for their preservation. In winter, the warmth of a number together will preserve their lives, while singly, they would probably perish. The power of fascination attributed to her, by a generous construction, may be understood to mean, that those who consider the liberty and blessings which America affords, and once come over to her, never afterwards leave her, but spend their lives with her. She strongly resembles America in this, that she is beautiful in youth and her beauty increaseth with her age.

Franklin signed the letter not with his own name but as "An American Guesser." Perhaps he was afraid of being identified as a troublemaker by the British. If the choice of our national symbol had been down to me, I'd definitely have gone with the turkey.

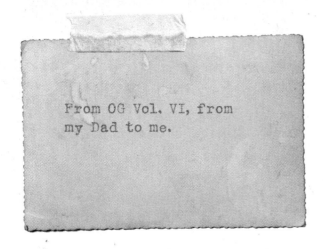

December 2011

Dear Charlie,

Every winter, flocks of starlings gather in the skies above Rome, wheeling, spinning, swooping, forming vast patterns in the sky. Watching them from my hotel window, I think of you on the porch on Raquette Lake gazing up into the sky. I think you'd love it here— pizza, ice cream, and birds to spot. During the day, the starlings forage in the countryside, but in the evenings they return to cavort above the building tops and roost. They are much more social than the solitary, mean-spirited eagle. A flock of starlings is called a "murmuration." When I mentioned the starlings to the manager of the hotel, she told me that Mozart had a pet starling that was said to be able to sing a few bars of his piano concerto in G major. Quite some bird!

Your father

163

Charles Whistler Esq.

Dear Charlie,

There are certain things we Whistlers expect from our 10-year-olds. We expect decent table manners. A reasonable handle on your multiplication tables. An ability to recognize the president of the United States. But perhaps most of all, we expect you to be able to hold your own with adults at the looming end-of-summer barbecue. In years past, it's been fine for you to skedaddle at the first sight of a grown-up. But those days are over. It's time to toughen up. (I sometimes think we take too long to toughen up children. In Iceland, where boys grow strong on pickled herring, roast whale, and putrid shark meat, mothers don't waste their time on lullabies about itsy-bitsy spiders. They go straight for the tough love: *Sofúr thu svid thitt / Svartur i áugum / Far i fulan pytt / Fullan af dráugum.* Translates as: *Sleep, you black-eyed pig / Fall into a deep pit full of ghosts.*)

I realize that there are few things a boy enjoys less than the company of adults he scarcely knows. Terms like "chitchat" and "small talk" mean nothing to him. All he can think at a grown-up party is "When can I get back to my room, or my friends, or anywhere but with these stiffs with their liquor and their cheese cubes?" But I'm afraid there's no getting away from these dreaded functions. They're a part of life. So let me give you a few pointers to ease the pain.

The first thing to understand is that there are very few people in this world who march fearlessly into every social encounter. Most of us are nervous wrecks, worried about what others will think of us. You'd think such anxiety would disappear with age. And it does. A bit. But just remind yourself that an adult presented with a young boy to talk to is likely just as worried as you are. They're thinking, what on earth do I talk to this ankle-biter about?

Second. The thing people love to talk about more than anything else is THEMSELVES. And the way to get them talking about themselves is to ask them questions. Ask them what they do for a job, how many children they have, where they are going for their vacation. If you really want to butter them up, ask them the secret of their success. This is the dreaded "small talk"—polite conversation about the basic facts of your everyday life. Don't worry if it seems boring to begin with, and don't object if people start to ask you similar questions about your school and your family. For all their adult smells and yellowing teeth, they're as flummoxed as you are.

With strangers, you've got to start somewhere and you might as well start with the obvious stuff. Then, if you find you are getting on well with someone and have things in common, you can gradually move on to more interesting, unusual things.

Above all, DON'T TRY TO BE GROWN-UP. Most adults spend their whole time with other adults who are grown-up and serious, and they love being with young people who look at the world in a different way. Have you ever noticed the way adults go on diets, dye their hair, and have plastic surgery? That's all for one reason—they want to be

young again. You've got the one thing they want—youth—so don't try to be old. You'll seem boring and ridiculous.

So there it is: be confident, be inquisitive, and act your age. Sip your root beer and soon, it'll all be over. I know you'll make me proud.

Your father

My Dad had paper-clipped to this letter two more items, which he'd picked out from earlier OGs. Clearly he wanted to make sure this vital Whistler wisdom wasn't forgotten. They're passages of advice on youth and manners by George Washington and Mark Twain.

When George Washington was 16, a schoolboy in Virginia, he found a 200-year-old list called 101 Rules of Civility & Decent Behavior in Company and Conversation, and copied it out. The language may be old-fashioned, but the advice is not. It's as valid for you as it was for young GW. I've taken out the stuff about when and how to doff one's hat, and whittled the rest down to what I thought essential.

> When in company, put not your hands to any part of the body not usually discovered.

> In the presence of others, sing not to yourself with a humming voice, or drum with your fingers or feet.

✍ Shake not the head, feet, or legs; roll not the eyes; lift not one eyebrow higher than the other, wry not the mouth, and bedew no man's face with your spittle by approaching too near him when you speak.

✍ Keep your nails clean and short, also your hands and teeth clean, yet without showing any great concern for them.

✍ Let your countenance be pleasant but in serious matters somewhat grave.

✍ Show not yourself glad at the misfortune of another though he were your enemy.

✍ Do not laugh too loud or too much at any public spectacle.

✍ Let your discourse with men of business be short and comprehensive.

✍ Strive not with your superior in argument, but always submit your judgment to others with modesty.

✍ Do not express joy before one sick in pain, for that contrary passion will aggravate his misery.

✍ When a man does all he can, though it succeed not well, blame not him that did it.

✍ Mock not nor jest at any thing of importance. Break no jests that are sharp, biting, and if you deliver any thing witty and pleasant, abstain from laughing thereat yourself.

✍ Be not hasty to believe flying reports to the disparagement of any.

✿ Wear not your clothes foul, or ripped, or dusty, but see they be brushed once every day at least and take heed that you approach not to any uncleanness.

✿ Associate yourself with men of good quality if you esteem your own reputation; for 'tis better to be alone than in bad company.

✿ A man ought not to value himself of his achievements or rare qualities of wit; much less of his riches, virtue, or kindred.

✿ Speak not injurious words neither in jest nor earnest; scoff at none although they give occasion.

✿ Think before you speak, pronounce not imperfectly, nor bring out your words too hastily, but orderly and distinctly.

✿ Undertake not what you cannot perform but be careful to keep your promise.

✿ Be not tedious in discourse, make not many digressions, nor repeat often the same manner of discourse.

✿ Speak not evil of the absent, for it is unjust.

✿ Being set at meat scratch not, neither spit, cough, or blow your nose except there's a necessity for it.

✿ Put not another bite into your mouth 'til the former be swallowed. Let not your morsels be too big for the jowls.

✿ Be not angry at table whatever happens and if you have reason to be so, show it not but on a cheerful countenance especially if there be strangers, for good humor makes one dish of meat a feast.

❧ Let your recreations be manful not sinful.

❧ Labor to keep alive in your breast that little spark of celestial fire called conscience.

Mark Twain had this Advice for Youth in 1882: Being told I would be expected to talk here, I inquired what sort of talk I ought to make. They said it should be something suitable to youth—something didactic, instructive, or something in the nature of good advice. Very well. I have a few things in my mind which I have often longed to say for the instruction of the young; for it is in one's tender early years that such things will best take root and be most enduring and most valuable. First, then, I will say to you my young friends—and I say it beseechingly, urgently:

Always obey your parents, when they are present. This is the best policy in the long run, because if you don't, they will make you. MOST PARENTS THINK THEY KNOW BETTER THAN YOU DO, AND YOU CAN GENERALLY MAKE MORE BY HUMORING THAT SUPERSTITION THAN YOU CAN BY ACTING ON YOUR OWN BETTER JUDGMENT.

BE RESPECTFUL TO YOUR SUPERIORS, if you have any, also to strangers, and sometimes to others. If a person offend you, and you are in doubt as to whether it was intentional or not, do not resort to extreme measures; simply watch your chance and hit him with a brick. That will be sufficient. If you shall find that he had not intended any offense, come out frankly and confess yourself in the wrong when you struck him; acknowledge it like a man and say you didn't mean to. Yes, always avoid violence; in this age of charity and kindliness, the time has gone by for such things. Leave dynamite to the low and unrefined.

Go to bed early, get up early—this is wise. Some authorities say get up with the sun; some say get up with one thing, others with another. But a lark is really the best thing to get up with. It gives you a splendid reputation with everybody to know that you get up with the lark; and if you get the right kind of lark, and work at him right, you can easily train him to get up at half past nine, every time—it's no trick at all.

Now as to the matter of lying. YOU WANT TO BE VERY CAREFUL ABOUT LYING; OTHERWISE YOU ARE NEARLY SURE TO GET CAUGHT. ONCE CAUGHT, YOU CAN NEVER AGAIN BE IN THE EYES TO THE GOOD AND THE PURE, WHAT YOU WERE BEFORE. Many a young person has injured himself permanently through a single clumsy and ill finished lie, the result of carelessness born of incomplete training. Some authorities hold that the young ought not to lie at all. That, of course, is putting it rather stronger than necessary; still while I cannot go quite so far as that, I do maintain, and I believe I am right, that the young ought to be temperate in the use of this great art until practice and experience shall give them that confidence, elegance, and precision which alone can make the accomplishment graceful and profitable. Patience, diligence, painstaking attention to detail—these are requirements; these, in time, will make the student perfect; upon these only, may he rely as the sure foundation for future eminence. Think what tedious years of study, thought, practice, experience, went to the equipment of that peerless old master who was able to impose upon the whole world the lofty and sounding maxim that "Truth is mighty and will prevail"—the most majestic compound fracture of fact which any of woman born has yet achieved. For the history of our race, and each individual's experience, are sewn thick with evidences that a truth is not hard to kill, and that a lie well told is immortal. There is in Boston a monument of the man who discovered anesthesia; many people are aware, in these latter days, that that man didn't discover it at all, but stole the discovery from another man. Is this truth mighty, and will it prevail? Ah no, my hearers, the monument is made of hardy material, but the lie it tells will outlast it a million years. An awkward, feeble, leaky lie is a thing which you ought to make it your unceasing study to avoid; such a lie as that has no more real permanence than an average truth. WHY, YOU MIGHT AS WELL TELL THE TRUTH AT ONCE AND BE DONE WITH IT. A feeble, stupid, preposterous lie will not live two years—except it be a slander upon somebody. It is indestructible then, of course, but that is no merit of yours. A final word: begin your practice of this gracious and beautiful art early— begin now. If I had begun earlier, I could have learned how.

NEVER HANDLE FIREARMS CARELESSLY. The sorrow and suffering that have been caused through the innocent but heedless handling of firearms by the young! Only four days ago, right in the next farm house to the one where I am spending the summer, a grandmother, old and gray and sweet, one of the loveliest spirits in the land, was sitting at her work, when her young grandson crept in and got down an old, battered, rusty gun which had not been touched for many years and was supposed not to be loaded, and pointed it at her, laughing and threatening to shoot. In her fright she ran screaming and pleading toward the door on the other side of the room; but as she passed him he placed the gun almost against her very breast and pulled the trigger! He had supposed it was not loaded. And he was right—it wasn't. So there wasn't any harm done. It is the only case of that kind I ever heard of. Therefore, just the same, don't you meddle with old unloaded firearms; they are the most deadly and unerring things that have ever been created by man. You don't have to take any pains at all with them; you don't have to have a rest, you don't have to have any sights on the gun, you don't have to take aim, even. No, you just pick out a relative and bang away, and you are sure to get him. A youth who can't hit a cathedral at thirty yards with a Gatling gun in three quarters of an hour, can take up an old empty musket and bag his grandmother every time, at a hundred. Think what Waterloo would have been if one of the armies had been boys armed with old muskets supposed not to be loaded, and the other army had been composed of their female relations. The very thought of it makes one shudder.

THERE ARE MANY SORTS OF BOOKS; BUT GOOD ONES ARE THE SORT FOR THE YOUNG TO READ. Remember that. They are a great, an inestimable, and unspeakable means of improvement. Therefore be careful in your selection, my young friends; be very careful; confine yourselves exclusively to Robertson's *Sermons*, Baxter's *Saints' Rest*, *The Innocents Abroad*, and works of that kind.

But I have said enough. I hope you will treasure up the instructions which I have given you, and make them a guide to your feet and a light to your understanding. Build your character thoughtfully and painstakingly upon these precepts, and by and by, when you have got it built, you will be surprised and gratified to see how nicely and sharply it resembles everybody else's.

THE RAQUETTE REPORTER

ELATED!

Longest Lake in Adirondacks Conquered by Mother of 3: Eats steak, Greases Up, and Swims into History

BY CHARLES WHISTLER
Special Correspondent

Not since the French blasted Fort William Henry with their cannons two hundred years ago has Lake George heard a sound like it heard on Saturday night. More than 10,000 people gathered along Beach Road to cheer and honk their car horns as Diane Struble, 25, pulled her exhausted body from Lake George. She had been swimming for more than 35 hours from one end of the lake to the other, the first person to complete this remarkable feat.

"MY GOSH THIS THING IS LONG!"
She was 147 pounds when she dived into the lake and 131 pounds when she

173

came out. For the first mile and a half she swam breaststroke, then the crawl the rest of the way. The doctors who examined her after her epic swim pronounced her in "excellent shape." Her three children were very relieved.

After several hours in the water, she told reporters, she thought to herself: "My gosh, this thing is long! What am I doing?" It was a question many of us had asked ourselves.

During the first night, the dauntless Struble swam the portion of the lake known as the narrows. The air temperature dropped to the low 40s and the people in the boats following her huddled together for warmth. "I had to swim hard or I would have stiffened up," she said.

At 3:00 a.m., though, she took a brief rest, devouring two hamburgers as she trod water.

TOUGH LEGS

Miss Struble taught herself to swim as an 8-year-old girl. She had been dreaming of swimming the length of Lake George for years. In August 1950, when she was 18, she made her first attempt. But a nasty storm whipped up the waves during the first 20 hours. She struggled through storms and thick fog, and her mother ordered her out of the water

after she had swum just over half the distance. A subsequent attempt in 1951 was also foiled by the weather.

During the intervening years, she built up her strength by running for miles along mountain trails and climbing the 2,000-foot Prospect Mountain three times a week. She also walked 25 miles a day from her home in Schenectady to Albany and back without ever accepting a ride.

Last year, she prepared for her big swim by swimming from the Sagamore

Hotel in Bolton to the village and back, about 24 miles. She toughened herself against the cold by spending winter nights in her sleeping bag in the snow. From early summer, she spent 8 hours a days swimming in Lake George.

Before diving into the water at 10:30 a.m. on Friday, she ate a large steak and then coated her body with five pounds of grease to protect her against the cold, spring-fed water. The water tem-

perature during her swim averaged 60 degrees.

She had plotted her route south from Ticonderoga to Lake George to take advantage of the prevailing winds. Her goal was to swim in as straight a line as possible and not be forced by the wind and currents into an exhausting zigzag. She knew, like every Lake George boater, how the lake can turn from placid to notorious white-capped fury in less than 20 minutes.

During rest periods, she joked with people on the boats following her. When the wind whipped up, she was handed a pair of goggles. As she swam on, word spread of her attempt and the crowd at Lake George grew. Bets were placed and a carnival atmosphere took over Beach Road. A mile from victory she was still going strong, her legs aching, but her resolve still strong.

Postscript

In 1959, Struble almost drowned as she swam from Burlington, Vermont, to Plattsburgh on the New York side of Lake Champlain. In August, she visited New York City and swam 30 miles around the island of Manhattan in 11 hours and 28 minutes.

From OG Vol. VI, August 2015.

We Whistlers love a story of victory against the odds. Like Diane Struble swimming the length of Lake George. I almost missed this postcard sent by Charles Watson Whistler to his son Charles Wilfred Whistler as it had tumbled under a chair.

May 1947

"Rockefeller Center is complete—and what a glorious place it is: 19 buildings surging out of the granite of this crowded little island of Manhattan. Hard to believe Mr. Rockefeller broke ground in 1930, just as the Great Depression overwhelmed America. Everyone thought he was crazy. But now that Rockefeller Center's a success, those same people are calling him a prophet. Amazing how persistence can change minds."

Then in my father's OG (Vol. V) I found a magazine article about Bethany Hamilton. She took toughness to a whole other level. She grew up in Hawaii, where kids surf the way kids in the rest of America play baseball or soccer. The moment class is out, they grab their boards and disappear out into the ocean. They paddle to where the waves break, dive into barrels of blue-green water, and pop up high on a cresting wall of water surfing back towards shore, screaming with delight.

Bethany was one of these kids, a "goofy-foot" surfer who pivoted her board with her left foot. By the time she was 13, she was winning surf contests against much older competitors. She was tipped to be one of the surfing greats. But at 7:30 a.m. on October 13, 2003, her life changed.

That morning she was picked up from school by her best friend Alana Blanchard, Alana's father Hoyt, and brother, Byron. They headed for the north shore of Kauai and paddled out about half a mile to West Reef, hoping to catch some of the giant, curling waves which had earned the area its nickname: Tunnels.

Bethany was paddling along in the calm water, when a tiger shark swam up and bit off her left arm, taking a chunk of her surfboard with it. There was no struggle or tugging at her flesh. The shark bit and disappeared, its bite so powerful and clean that Bethany did not even notice her arm was gone until she saw the water all round her turning red.

"I think a shark just attacked me," she said quietly to Alana, who screamed for help. Hoyt acted quickly, pulling off his Lycra vest and wrapping it around the four inches left of Bethany's arm to stanch the bleeding. Then he had to decide. Did he send the three children back to shore and stay here to fend off the sharks, which would be attracted by all the blood? Or did they all stay close and head for shore together? Hoyt called to Byron and they tied a surf leash to Bethany's board so they could pull it. Alana paddled alongside talking to her friend to keep her conscious.

When they reached shore, a paramedic who had been snorkeling nearby lashed another surf leash tight around Bethany's arm. They lifted her on the surfboard into the back of Hoyt's truck and headed for a hospital.

By the time she got there, she had lost over 60 percent of her blood. The cut was so clean, the doctor thought Bethany's arm had been surgically amputated.

The bite mark on the board was 16 inches long and 8 inches wide.

When word spread about the attack, a couple of local surfers and fishermen, Bill Hamilton and Ralph Young, decided to set out in pursuit of the shark. There had been other reports of the shark cruising the area and frightening swimmers. Hawaiian fishermen don't like to kill sharks. But in this case, Bill and Ralph felt it was necessary.

They built a huge floating rig out of three separate buoys lashed together by an inner tube. It was strong enough to hold an 1,800-pound shark, or 10 men. For bait they used a 5-foot gray shark concealing a hook the size of a basketball.

Two weeks after the attack on Bethany, they hauled in a 14-foot tiger shark. When they opened up its belly, they found no sign of Bethany's arm or surfboard. But when they cut out its jaw to measure it, they found it was 18 inches across between the tips of its mouth and matched perfectly to the teeth marks left on the board. No one doubted that this was the beast.

They gave a strip of the shark's skin to the local Kahuna tribe, who stretched it across a drum and beat it in prayer to the spirits who calm the seas.

Bethany was back in the water a month later and soon competing again. She hopes the story of her attack and recovery will inspire others never to give up in the face of the most terrifying odds.

My Dad had attached to the story about Bethany a school essay by his grandfather about Brook Watson, who was born in England in 1735. Different

century, same shark troubles. By the time Brook was 6, both of his parents had died, so like many boys at the time, he joined the crew of a merchant ship and set sail. One day, in 1749, his ship was anchored in Havana harbor. The warm Caribbean water was irresistible, and Brook decided to strip off and dive in. He swam away from the ship, relishing the exercise after so many days at sea.

Tiger sharks are among the strongest and most vicious predators in the sea. They don't just eat turtles, fish, debris, and anything they can fit inside their vast jaws. They even eat other sharks. A fleshy young lad splashing alone in the water? Well, that may as well have been chocolate cake.

Brook's crewmates saw the shark's fin circling the boy, screamed, and leaped into a boat to save him. But the shark was faster. It locked its teeth around Brook's right leg, stripped away the flesh from his knee to his foot, and dragged him beneath the waves.

The crew raced to where Brook had vanished, searching for his body. Two minutes later, Brook popped to the surface a hundred yards away. The crew pulled on their oars, but again they were too slow. Brook disappeared, hauled down by the shark. The crew scanned every inch of the water, searching for their friend. One of them seized a hook and took up a position in the bow, ready to strike the beast if it reappeared.

Every second they waited seemed like an hour. They struggled to keep their balance as the boat was rolled by the waves.

All of a sudden Brook popped up, naked, bleeding, lying on the surface of the water. The shark made another lunge towards him. The crewman with the hook thrust down hard on the shark's nose and drove it away. Two others reached into the water, and pulled Brook in, heaving his exhausted body over the side of the boat. He was white from the loss of blood. His right foot was gone, the flesh and muscle of his right calf shorn away to the bone.

The crew bound his wounds and rushed him to shore. The combination of seawater and blood loss should have killed him. But miraculously, after his leg was amputated beneath the knee, he recovered and lived the rest of his life with a wooden stump from his right knee down.

He became a successful merchant, Lord Mayor of London, and was made a baronet, which entitled him to create his own motto and coat of arms. He chose the Latin motto *"Scuto Divino,"* which means "Under God's Protection" and explained how he survived. At the top of his coat of arms, he put Neptune, the god of the sea, fending off a shark with his trident. And in the top left corner of the shield, he placed a severed foot.

The American painter John Singleton Copley read of Watson's story while visiting London in 1778 and decided to make a painting of it. Watson bought it, and when he died he left it to Christ's Hospital, a boys' school in London. He wrote that he hoped the picture and the long, successful, and happy life he lived after he was attacked would serve as a "most usefull Lesson to Youth."

From OG Vol. VI, August 2015.

All this talk of Teddy Roosevelt and victory against the odds might make life on Raquette Lake seem all "bully" and "rah-rah." Luckily it's not. One of the best things about it is that the time up here is your own. There is no bell clanging at 7:30 a.m., no drills to be done before breakfast, no homework, no lame group craft projects. Most days you're woken up by a squirrel scampering across the roof of your bedroom. You stroll out onto the porch in your pajamas. Stretch. Flop into a chair. Listen to the loons. Peer through your binoculars to see a couple more birds. And if you're feeling really industrious, pick up a book or a sketchpad.

Whistlers have always been enthusiastic sketchers and painters—some good, some not so good, but always enthusiastic. By the end of each summer, that refrigerator door of ours is thick with doodles, so thick several flutter away each time you open the door to get milk. And every week my Mom or Dad puts a new postcard of a work of art on the bulletin board beside the screen door.

Sometimes I barely notice it. Other times I can't get it out of my mind, like this one by the Dutch painter Vermeer called *The Little Street*. It seems so boring at first, just a street, some houses. All so precise. But I keep looking at the doorway, down the alleyway, over the rooftops, wanting to know what's there. What's going on behind the windows? What's in the sacks lying beside the street? It's like the start of a mystery story, completely still but on the brink of something. Who knows what's really going on here? I can't stop thinking about it. As I dug through the various Omnium Gatherums, I found stacks of notes and thoughts about art. Turns out we've been trying to figure it all out for decades.

July 1954

One of the hardest things about any kind of art is getting started. It's easy to be scared off by the empty page, the empty canvas, to imagine that whatever mark you make on it has to be a mark of genius. Hogwash! The trick is to plunge in, just like you cannonball into the lake that first day of summer. If you dipped your toe in and pulled it out again and shivered and worried, you'd never get in. But if you just charge down the dock and leap in, screaming at the thrill of the brisk unknown, the shock of the cold is quickly replaced by excitement that summer is finally here.

Take Winston Churchill. Now here is a man who has achieved more than most. Helping to win the Second World War as Britain's prime minister is just part of it. He has written more than 40 books and won the Nobel Prize for Literature. But all that success hasn't saved him from suffering terrible periods of gloom, which he calls the "black dog." He battles through them with his enthusiasms. He has learned to lay brick. He reads avidly. But his greatest passion is painting, which he took up late in life and with great trepidation. Learning to paint is not easy at any time, and even the great Churchill, who could command armies and address thousands, wrote that initially he was terrified by the blank canvas.

He bought a canvas and paints and stared at the empty sheet and the glistening palette. He tried painting the sky, mixing blue and white and dabbing tentatively at the canvas. For a man so decisive in matters of politics and war, the challenge of painting proved surprisingly intimidating. Just then, the wife of a painter friend drove up to his house and observed his hesitancy. She strode up to his easel, seized his brushes and paints and began smearing the canvas with broad, confident strokes. The canvas did not bite back. It meekly took whatever was smeared across it. Churchill took heart. He no longer quailed at the empty canvas. He became its master, painting whatever he chose. He attacked it with what he described as a "berserk fury" reveling in the feel of the brush, the smell of the paint and all the creative possibilities which lay before him.

August 1956

Just as most writers are voracious readers and note-takers, artists are compulsive observers and sketchers. You can see in their sketches how hard they work to become any good. It's through all this endless doodling that they develop their skills. In 1637, an elephant called Hansken visited Amsterdam. One of the many who saw her was the artist Rembrandt, who made four sketches of her in chalk.

Artists also work on their craft through "schemata" or variations on very simple things like ears or noses or hats. So when they paint a picture, they have in mind dozens of faces which they have practiced in different forms and then pick specific items from these schemata to assemble new pictures. Learning schemata is like learning scales when you play a musical instrument. You don't learn them for their own sake, but in order to make yourself a better musician, comfortable with any arrangement of notes.

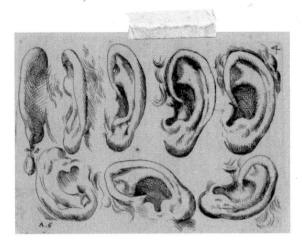

And even when you're really good, the hard work doesn't stop. John Constable was an English painter who loved the countryside where he grew up. He once wrote to a friend: "The sound of water escaping from the mill-dams etc., willows, old rotten planks, slimy posts and brick work—I love such things. . . . Painting is with me but another word for feeling, and I associate my 'careless boyhood' with all that lies on the banks of the Stour. These scenes made me a painter, and I am grateful." I'm no Constable, but I feel the same way about the Adirondacks. It's here on the rotten planks of a familiar dock beside the lake I love that I feel most grateful. Constable was a compulsive sketcher and one of his favorite guides to drawing was by Alexander Cozens. Even when his fame was ensured, he would work on copying Cozens's depictions of the sky and then create his own. He called this "skying."

Half Cloud Half Plain, the Lights of the Clouds Lighter, and the Shades Darker than the Plain Part and Darker at the Top than the Bottom. The Tint Twice Over in the Plain Part, and Twice in the Clouds.

All Cloudy, except a Narrow Opening at the Bottom of the Sky, with Others Smaller, the Clouds Darker than the Plain Part; and Darker at the Top than the Bottom. The Tint Twice Over.

189

TARJETA POSTAL

My Mom is a painter, and a few years
ago she told me she was unhappy with
what she was painting and wrote to
my Dad about how artists search for
inspiration. She said that writing
it all down was helpful. I found the
letters she wrote to Dad in OG Vol. V.

May 2006

M W

Dear Charlie,

It's one thing knowing how to draw. It's another thing knowing what to draw. When she was a child, Beatrix Potter used to draw insects and animals. Later in life when she wrote about Peter Rabbit and Jeremy Fisher, she had no trouble imagining the details of their lives. Others have to go farther afield to find inspiration. Brice Marden is a painter who lives in New York. In 1994, he visited the Dunhuang caves in northwest China. These caves are surrounded by the Taklamakan Desert, and their walls are covered in murals painted over centuries by Buddhist monks and pilgrims. Many of the murals show dancers twirling ribbons. When Marden returned home, he was inspired by the ribbon paintings and Chinese calligraphy to paint a series of canvases using long ailanthus sticks which he found on the streets of New York, instead of brushes. This meant he could paint at the same distance from the canvas as a viewer would stand. It also forced him to move more, to mimic the movements of the dancers.

His paintings are often around the same height as an average adult so that they feel like companions in a room rather than soulless objects. Marden once said, "What I like is when I see paintings of mine that I just don't understand." Most artists I know aren't so confident.

Willem de Kooning said that he found inspiration for his paintings when falling or slipping. He said it was a "wonderful sensation . . . to slip into this glimpse," to lose control for an instant, and then to convey that fleeting moment on canvas. The Californian painter Wayne Thiebaud can look at a plain old frosted cake or ice cream cone and think it worthy of his brush. During the 1960s, Claes Oldenburg made sculptures inspired by hamburgers. Hamburgers!!!! He said: "The hamburger is a perfectly structural piece of food and I think I'd almost rather look at it than eat it. It's got three circles—top half of the bun, patty and bottom half; and if you put an onion slice on it you have even more variation. A pickle is very geometrical too." All right, Claes.

Others search harder for inspiration. On the bright morning of April 10th, 1927, Ansel Adams and four friends set off to take photographs of Half Dome, the mountain which dominates the Yosemite Valley. Adams was 28 years old, skinny, with an off-center nose, broken when he was thrown into the air during the great San Francisco earthquake of 1906. He wore a leather jacket, a pair of jeans, a fedora hat against the sun, and black basketball sneakers to help him keep his footing on the slippery rock path. He carried his cameras, lenses, and tripod in a pack on his back.

Adams had loved the High Sierra and Yosemite since he was a teenager. His parents worried that he was thin and weak, so they sent him off hiking in the High Sierra with his uncle Frank. Every day, they ate oatmeal and flapjacks for breakfast. They fished for trout and ate it for supper, flavored with wild onion. By the time Ansel returned, he was tanned and healthy, and had fallen in love with the wild mountains of California. He returned many times to this wilderness with just his camera and what he considered his essentials: "salt, sugar, bacon, flour, jelly beans and whiskey."

That April morning, he and his friends started along the Glacier Point trail on the floor of the Valley and then began the steep climb towards Sierra Point. It was a long scramble from there to the Diving Board, an outcrop of rock some 4,000 feet above the Valley. They made it there around lunchtime. Adams set up his camera and at 2:30 p.m., just as the sun hit the face of Half Dome, he took his picture. He used a deep red filter to turn the sky dark and velvety, to create a more intense contrast with the sunlit rock. It wasn't just a point and click which led to that photograph. It involved perspiration and skill, and a deeply felt childhood memory.

And then there are those inspirations which just come barging in on you, when you're not even looking. You ever read how William Carlos Williams was walking along a New York street on his way to see his friend, the painter Marsden Hartley, and a fire engine passed by, its bells clanging, the number five painted in gold on its side? He was so startled, he seized a piece of paper from his pocket and wrote a short poem.

That poem, "The Great Figure," was published in 1921:

Among the rain

and lights

I saw the figure 5

in gold

on a red

fire truck

moving

tense

unheeded

to gong clangs

siren howls

and wheels rumbling

through the dark city

Eight years later, Charles Demuth was inspired by the poem to paint *The Figure 5 in Gold*. Both Williams and Demuth were trying to capture that sense of standing on the sidewalk watching a bright, noisy fire engine hurtling past.

Two great works of art from a single stroll. That's inspiration in itself. Why is it so darned hard for me?

With love,
Meg

This letter came from OG Vol. V. It was written to my Great-Uncle Robert, who was eighteen at the time and thinking of going into politics as a career after college. Charles Wilfred's brother, Teddy, was a Communist who lived in the West Village of New York City. He only ever came to the Adirondacks under extreme family pressure, and even then he moped on the porch. He found nature threatening and boring. He much preferred the city. He died before I was born, but the pictures of him show a man with gray hair swept back over his collar, and a cowboy's faraway look. He claimed to be a poet, though he never published a poem. Didn't matter, my father said. He lived a poet's life. He read, he talked, he listened to music, and his neighbors loved him. When Teddy heard of Robert's political ambitions, he wrote to try to keep him on track.

From OG Vol. V

TEDDY WHISTLER
21 Bethune Street
New York, NY
June 7, 1968

Robert,

A priest once told me that we should all walk around with two pieces of paper in our pockets, one on the left, one on the right. On one you write, "Today is all about you, wonderful you." And on the other, you write, "You are nothing more than a meaningless speck of dust in the great cosmic farce." I thought about this today when I woke up and read the news from California, of Robert Kennedy's assassination.

It is a tragedy, of course. Such violence towards a man with a wife and children, who was clearly loved by so many. Every politician has enemies, and I've read he had plenty. But we are supposed to live in a democracy, not a world of gangster blood feuds. Whether we knew or cared for Kennedy or not, his murder feels like a curse on all of us.

Yet, think of what the priest said. The world is full of violence, so little of which reaches our eyes and ears. We rage against what we choose to rage against, but remain indifferent to so much. So why do we care about Kennedy? Why this speck of dust and not another?

Now you know I don't care much for politics. I know that we Whistlers have a cultish thing for Teddy Roosevelt. I'm the only one in the family who doesn't. But I hold my tongue, else I'll be called a Communist and get a face full of blueberry pie. But let me tell you, in the strict confines of this letter, that I find all that "bully" Roosevelt stuff to be nonsense. He was a warmonger, a bully in the schoolyard sense. One day, I hope, you'll read of the terrible violence he supported in the Philippines and see that all that manly vigor had its dark side. Many fine words are spoken to justify wars and violence, but in the end all wars are wars on children. Create all the national parks you like, doesn't change it.

So why did the news of Kennedy's death so darken my breakfast? It was a speech he made a couple of months ago in Indianapolis. I still have the clipping from the *Times* tacked up above my desk. It was the night of April 4th, 1968, and he was just three weeks into his campaign for the presidency. As he left for Indianapolis, news reached him of the shooting of Martin Luther King Jr.

Kennedy's staff advised him to cancel the speech. They feared there would be riots as people expressed their anger. It would not be safe, they warned. But Kennedy was adamant. When he landed, he learned that King was dead. He insisted on being taken to the planned site of his speech, in one of the poorest parts of the city. It was home to many

African Americans, to whom King had been a hero.

Five years ago, as you know, Robert's brother, President John F. Kennedy, was assassinated. Robert had never spoken publicly of it. But if ever there was a moment to draw on that experience, to make a stand against those who thought murder and violence were the best way to annihilate the good in a society, now was it. It was evening and the crowd was restless. Kennedy spoke briefly from notes he had scribbled during his flight and drive into the city. Here's what he said:

Ladies and Gentlemen: I'm only going to talk to you just for a minute or so this evening, because I have some very sad news for all of you—Could you lower those signs, please?—I have some very sad news for all of you, and, I think, sad news for all of our fellow citizens, and people who love peace all over the world; and that is that Martin Luther King was shot and was killed tonight in Memphis, Tennessee.

Martin Luther King dedicated his life to love and to justice between fellow human beings. He died in the cause of that effort. In this difficult day, in this difficult time for the United States, it's perhaps well to ask what

kind of a nation we are and what direction we want to move in. For those of you who are black—considering the evidence evidently is that there were white people who were responsible—you can be filled with bitterness, and with hatred, and a desire for revenge.

We can move in that direction as a country, in greater polarization—black people amongst blacks, and white amongst whites, filled with hatred toward one another. Or we can make an effort, as Martin Luther King did, to understand, and to comprehend, and replace that violence, that stain of bloodshed that has spread across our land, with an effort to understand, compassion and love.

For those of you who are black and are tempted to be filled with hatred and mistrust of the injustice of such an act, against all white people, I would only say that I can also feel in my own heart the same kind of feeling. I had a member of my family killed, but he was killed by a white man.

But we have to make an effort in the United States, we have to make an effort to understand, to get beyond, or go beyond these rather difficult times.

My favorite poem, my favorite poet was Aeschylus. And he once wrote:

EVEN IN OUR SLEEP, PAIN WHICH CANNOT FORGET
FALLS DROP BY DROP UPON THE HEART,
UNTIL, IN OUR OWN DESPAIR,
AGAINST OUR WILL, COMES WISDOM
THROUGH THE AWFUL GRACE OF GOD.

What we need in the United States is not division; what we need in the United States is not hatred; what we need in the United States is not violence and lawlessness, but is love and wisdom, and compassion toward one another, and a feeling of justice toward those who still suffer within our country, whether they be white or whether they be black.

So I ask you tonight to return home, to say a prayer for the family of Martin Luther King—yeah, it's true—but more importantly to say a prayer for our own country, which all of us love—a prayer for understanding and that compassion of which I spoke.

We can do well in this country. We will have difficult times. We've had difficult times in the past. And we will have difficult times in the future. It is not the end of violence; it is not the end of lawlessness; and it's not the end of disorder.

But the vast majority of white people and the vast majority of black people in this country want to live together, want to improve the quality of our life, and want justice for all human beings that abide in our land.

Let us dedicate ourselves to what the Greeks wrote so many years ago: to tame the savageness of man and make gentle the life of this world. Let us dedicate ourselves to that, and say a prayer for our country and for our people.

Thank you very much.

And with that, he got back on his plane and flew away. There were no riots in Indianapolis last night.

If ever you do become a politician, make one speech like that and I'll forgive you your choice of career.

Your Commie Uncle,
Ted

From OG Vol. VI.

August 2015

Way back in the very earliest days of the Omnium Gatherum, Charles Wilberforce Whistler noted that President James Buchanan kept a Newfoundland named Lara. Ever since then, a list has been passed from OG to OG, updated with every president, listing the first family's pets. Even if we don't know much else about political history, at least we'll know the important stuff: that Dwight Eisenhower kept a Weimaraner called Heidi and Jimmy Carter's daughter, Amy, had a Siamese cat called Misty Malarky Ying Yang. When the rain falls in August and we're stuck inside, it's the basis for a memory game. Come on now, quick: which president kept a Norwegian elkhound called Weejie? (*Answer: Herbert Hoover.*)

BARACK OBAMA (2009–2016)

Bo and Sunny, Portuguese water dogs

GEORGE W. BUSH (2001–2009)

Spot Fetcher, English springer spaniel, one of Millie's puppies (see George H. W. Bush below)

Barney and Miss Beazley, Scottish terriers

India or Willie, cat, named after Texas baseball player Rubén Sierra, aka El Indio

Ofelia, longhorn cow

BILL CLINTON (1993–2001)

Socks the cat

Buddy, chocolate Labrador retriever

GEORGE H. W. BUSH (1989–1993)

Millie, springer spaniel

Ranger, one of Millie's puppies

RONALD REAGAN (1981–1989)

Lucky, Bouvier des Flandres

Rex, a Cavalier King Charles spaniel

Dogs and horses at ranch

JIMMY CARTER (1977–1981)

Grits, dog given to daughter Amy by her teacher and later returned

Misty Malarky Ying Yang, Amy Carter's Siamese cat

203

GERALD FORD (1974–1977)

Liberty, golden retriever

Shan, Siamese cat

RICHARD NIXON (1969–1974)

Checkers, cocker spaniel

Vicky, poodle

Pasha, terrier

King Timahoe, Irish setter

LYNDON JOHNSON (1963–1969)

Beagle and Little Beagle and Him and Her, all beagles

Blanco, a white collie

Yuki, mongrel dog

Hamsters and lovebirds

JOHN KENNEDY (1961–1963)

Charlie, Caroline Kennedy's Welsh terrier

Tom Kitten, a cat

Robin, a canary

Bluebell and Marybelle, parakeets

Macaroni, Caroline Kennedy's pony

Tex and Leprechaun, ponies

Debbie and Billie, hamsters

Pushinka (mutt), Charlie (Welsh terrier), Shannon (Irish cocker spaniel), Wolf (mutt, possibly part wolfhound and schnauzer), and Clipper (German shepherd), all dogs

Butterfly, White Tips, Blackie, and Streaker, all offspring of Pushinka and Charlie

Zsa Zsa, a rabbit; and Sardar, Jacqueline Kennedy's horse

DWIGHT EISENHOWER (1953–1961)

Heidi, Weimaraner

HARRY TRUMAN (1945–1953)

Feller, cocker spaniel

Mike, Margaret Truman's Irish setter

FRANKLIN D. ROOSEVELT (1933–1945)

Major, German shepherd

Meggie, Scottish terrier

Winks, Llewellyn setter

Tiny, Old English sheepdog

President, Great Dane

Faithful and loyal famous companion, Fala, the Scottish terrier

Blaze, Elliott Roosevelt's mastiff

FDR with Anna, his daughter, and her prize-winning Shepherd, Chief of the Mohawk.

HERBERT HOOVER (1929–1933)

King Tut and Pat, German shepherds

Big Ben and Sonnie, fox terriers

Glen, Scotch collie

Yukòn, Eskimo dog

Patrick, Irish wolfhound

Eaglehurst Gillette, setter

Weejie, Norwegian elkhound

CALVIN COOLIDGE (1923–1929)

Rob Roy and Prudence Prim, white collies

Paul Pry, Airedale

Calamity Jane, Shetland sheepdog

Boston Beans, bulldog

Palo Alto, bird dog

Rebecca and Horace, raccoons

Ebeneezer, donkey

Enoch, goose

Smoky, bobcat

Tiger, cat (stray)

Wallaby

Two lion cubs

Antelope

Pygmy hippo

WARREN HARDING (1921–1923)

Laddie Boy, Airedale

WOODROW WILSON (1913–1921)

Old Ike, ram

Puffins, cat

Mountain Boy, greyhound

Bruce, bull terrier

Songbirds

Sheep, on the White House lawn

WILLIAM TAFT (1909–1913)

Caruso, dog

Mooly Wooly and Pauline Wayne, cows

THEODORE ROOSEVELT (1901–1909)

Pete, bull terrier

Skip, rat terrier

Blackjack, Manchester terrier

Manchu, Pekingese

Rollo, Saint Bernard

Sailor Boy, Chesapeake Bay retriever

Tom Quartz and Slippers, cats

Emily Spinach, garter snake

Algonquin, pony

Maude, pig

Josiah, badger

Jonathan, piebald rat

Dr. Johnson, Bishop Doane, Fighting Bob Evans, and Father O'Grady, guinea pigs

Baron Spreckle, hen

Eli Yale, macaw

A one-legged rooster

WILLIAM MCKINLEY (1897–1901)
Washington Post, yellow-headed Mexican parrot

Valeriano Weyler and Enrique DeLome, Angora kittens

Roosters

BENJAMIN HARRISON (1889–1893)
His Whiskers, goat

Dash, collie

Mr. Reciprocity and Mr. Protection, opossums

GROVER CLEVELAND (1885–1889)
Mockingbird

CHESTER A. ARTHUR (1881–1885)
None

JAMES A. GARFIELD (1881)
Veto, dog

207

RUTHERFORD B. HAYES (1877—1881)

Dot, cocker spaniel

Hector, Newfoundland

Deke, English mastiff

Juno and Shep, hunting dogs

Grim, greyhound

Jet, dog

Piccolomini, cat

Miss Pussy, Siamese cat

ULYSSES S. GRANT (1869—1877)

Cincinnatus, St. Louis, Egypt, Reb, Billy Button, Butcher Boy, and Jeff Davis (his wartime mount), horses

Rosie, dog

ANDREW JOHNSON (1865—1869)

White mice he found in his bedroom

ABRAHAM LINCOLN (1861—1865)

Nanny and Nanko, goats

Jack, turkey

Fido, dog

Horse

JAMES BUCHANAN (1857—1861)

Lara, Newfoundland

Punch, toy-size terrier

FRANKLIN PIERCE (1853—1857)

Miniature Oriental dogs

Birds from Japan

MILLARD FILLMORE (1850—1853)

None

ZACHARY TAYLOR (1849—1850)

Old Whitey, horse

JAMES K. POLK (1845—1849)

Horse

JOHN TYLER (1841—1845)

Le Beau, Italian greyhound

Johnny Ty, canary

The General, horse

WILLIAM HENRY HARRISON (1841)

Sukey, cow

Goat

MARTIN VAN BUREN (1837–1841)

Briefly owned two tiger cubs

ANDREW JACKSON (1829–1837)

Pol, parrot (was taught to swear)

Fighting cocks

Horses

JOHN QUINCY ADAMS (1825–1829)

Alligator

Silkworms

JAMES MONROE (1817–1825)

Spaniel

JAMES MADISON (1809–1817)

Parrot, macaw

THOMAS JEFFERSON (1801–1809)

Dick, mockingbird

Buzzy and unknown, briards (dogs)

JOHN ADAMS (1797–1801)

Juno and Satan, dogs

Cleopatra, horse

GEORGE WASHINGTON (1789–1797)

Sweet Lips, Scentwell, and Vulcan, staghounds

Drunkard, Taster, Tipler, and Tipsy, black-and-tan hounds

Royal Gift, jackass

Nelson, horse

Well, Charlie, here it is, the old dollar bill, the greenback, bone, buck, spondoolick, smackeroo. Now, I'll want this one returned. But take a look. See what a busy scrap of paper it is, seething with patterns, symbols, numbers—and the glowering eye of Providence. I know how a dollar can ball up in your pockets, Charlie. How you can let a few turn to mush in the washing machine. So I thought you should know that there's some meaning to these things beyond how much ice cream they buy at Fat Bob's in Long Lake.

On one side, we have George Washington, Founder of the Nation, our first president and the owner of a

211

fine set of wooden teeth. This side of the note is the most technical. To the right of GW we have the seal of the U.S. Treasury. Just below that is the signature of the Secretary of the Treasury at the time the note was printed.

The Federal Reserve System is the central bank of the United States and, among other things, makes sure there is enough currency and coin to go around. There are 12 banks in the system, each with its own code number and letter. You see the four number twelves, two on each side of the note? That tells you which bank in the Federal Reserve issued the note. Try matching the number to the bank:

🖐 1	Boston	A	
🖐 2	New York	B	
🖐 3	Philadelphia	C	
🖐 4	Cleveland	D	
🖐 5	Richmond	E	
🖐 6	Atlanta	F	
🖐 7	Chicago	G	
🖐 8	St. Louis	H	
🖐 9	Minneapolis	I	
🖐 10	Kansas City	J	
🖐 11	Dallas	K	
🖐 12	San Francisco	L	

The big letter L in what looks like a bottle cap next to the 12 also tells you which bank issued the note. The bank's name is written right there in a circle in the bottle cap, San Francisco. Every single note has its own serial number, consisting of a letter, eight digits, and another letter. The first letter confirms which bank in the Federal Reserve issued the note, L again. The last letter tells you how many times the Bureau of Engraving and Printing used this sequence of numbers. G means this is the seventh run of this sequence. The letter and number H3 to the left of the number 12 tells you where on the printing plate this note was printed. Each plate looks like this:

A1	E1	A3	E3
B1	F1	B3	F3
C1	G1	C3	B3
D1	H1	D3	H3
A2	E2	A4	E4
B2	D2	B4	F3
C2	G2	C4	G4
D2	H2	D4	H4

The other side of the note shows the two sides of the seal of the United States, settled on after much haggling on June 20, 1782. To the left is a pyramid, and hovering above it an eye. The pyramid, a symbol of strength and longevity, is made up of 13 steps. These signify the 13 states in the original United States. The pyramid is unfinished, because the work of creating the United States will never be finished. (Imagine living in a country, or even being the kind of person, which thought itself so perfect there was nothing more to be done. How arrogant and dull would that be? Walt Whitman put it, more juicily: "To be ripe beyond further increase is to prepare to die.")

The eye belongs to Providence watching over the country. Beneath it are the words *"Annuit Coeptis,"* Latin for "It [Providence] Has Favored Our Undertakings." (Other ideas kicked around were "Rebellion to Tyrants Is Obedience to God" and *"Deo Favente,"* "With God's Favor.") At the base of the pyramid is the date MDCCLXXVI, 1776, the year of the Declaration of Independence. Beneath that the words *"Novus Ordo Seclorum,"* a "New Order of the Ages."

To the right is a bald eagle, the symbol of the United States. The eagle stands alone, with no visible means of support, showing how the United States is a self-reliant country. On the eagle's chest is a shield with thirteen stripes, bound by a band along the top. The 13 stripes are the states; the band represents Congress, which unifies them. Above it is a constellation of 13 stars. In one talon, the eagle grasps an olive branch with 13 leaves. In the other it holds 13 arrows. These symbolize the power of Congress to make war and peace. The motto above, *"E Pluribus Unum"*—13 letters—means "From Many, One," and was coined by Thomas Jefferson.

The phrase "In God We Trust" was added in 1957.

The first $1 bills issued by the federal government in 1862 featured a portrait of Secretary of the Treasury Salmon P. Chase. They quickly twigged that no one knew who this Salmon goon was and replaced him with George Washington. And so it has remained. The $2 has Thomas

Jefferson, the $5 Abraham Lincoln, the $10 Alexander Hamilton, the $20 Andrew Jackson, the $50 Ulysses Grant, and the $100 Benjamin Franklin. The Treasury used to print notes up to $100,000, which showed Woodrow Wilson, the 28th president. But now it stops at $100, the C-note, the Benjamin Franklin.

Finally a few words on spotting a counterfeit note. (Stopping counterfeiters was the original purpose of the Secret Service. They only got into presidential protection after Abraham Lincoln was shot.) Real dollars aren't completely smooth. They feel a little rough to the touch. Woven through the paper are colored filaments, which add to the texture. The portraits are sharply detailed. Run a fingernail across them to feel their bumps and ridges. Higher-denomination notes have watermarks of the person whose portrait is on the bill. You can see the watermarks if you hold the notes up to the light. On more recent bills worth $10 and up, you'll notice the color of the ink change from green to black or from copper to green as you look at them from different angles. If anyone gives you a note which feels too flat or lacks these details, hand it back with a "no thanks" and walk away. But don't assume they're the counterfeiter. They may just have been fooled themselves.

So spend some time with the dollar, Charlie. Study it. Feel it. Don't ball it up and ruin it. It takes effort to make one, and more to earn one.

With love,
Your father

7th August 1974

FRANCIS R. WHISTLER

Dear Charlie,

Whoooooooooaaaaah!

You're probably wondering what possessed me, your sensible kid brother, this fine reliable Whistler, to tightrope-walk across Fifth Avenue. If it was the spirit of adventure, then hallelujah! If the devil, then so be it. All I can say is that if you haven't seen Manhattan from 200 feet up on a bouncing wire—you haven't seen Manhattan. Even better than sprinting along the ridge of the cabin and diving head-first into Raquette Lake.

One morning, I was sitting in my office at the publishing company. I'd come in a few minutes early, poured myself a cup of coffee, and was staring at the stack of manuscripts on my desk. I leaned back, twirled my red pen between my fingers, and looked out of the window. I love New York. But that day, I didn't want to be there. I wanted to be hiking with you up to Lake Tear-of-the-Clouds, or standing in a river with a fly rod. Anything but sitting in a chair reading and editing other people's words. When I feel like this, my right leg starts to jiggle, and that morning it

217

was going up and down like a jackhammer. That's when my pal George stuck his head round my door—well, he stuck a newspaper round the door followed by his giant head.

"You see it? You see it?" he said. George tends to repeat himself when excited.

"See what?"

"The crazy Frenchman. Walked between the Twin Towers."

"What do you mean between them? Anyone can walk between them."

"Not down on the plaza, you ape. He shot a tightrope between the tops of them."

I leaped out of my seat and grabbed the paper. Philippe Petit, 24 years old, four years younger than me and a million times braver. One photograph showed him standing with his balancing bar waiting to step out over the void. Another had him walking across. The report explained why and how he had done it.

Six years before, he'd been sitting in his dentist's waiting room in Paris, browsing through magazines, when he saw pictures of the yet-to-be-completed towers. He stopped thinking of his toothache. "They called me," he told the newspaper. "I didn't choose them. Anything that is giant and man-made strikes me in an awesome way and calls me. I could secretly put my wire between the highest towers in the world. It was something that had to be done, and I couldn't explain it. It was a calling of the romantic type."

You bet it was! Most of us see a picture in a magazine and think, maybe, "Huh, interesting" and turn the page. Not this guy. He sees a construction project and thinks, "Now there's a challenge to my tightrope skills!" He ripped the page from the dentist's magazine and for the next six years plotted his stunt.

A few weeks ago, he arrived in New York for the first time in his life. Imagine that. First time in his life, and his mission is to walk between the towers. All most visitors want to do is go up the Empire State Building and eat a hot dog from a cart. He spent his time scouting out the towers, figuring out how to get to the top and walk across them before anyone could stop him. They don't issue permits for this. He even pretended to be a journalist so he could interview the manager of the World Trade Center. Now, that takes some nerve.

He had assembled a group of five, including himself. They gathered at the foot of the towers on the evening before the walk. Two went to the top of the North Tower while Philippe and two others climbed the South Tower. They carried their equipment in ordinary-looking bags. The moment they could, they slipped out of sight of the security guards and sneaked up to the roof.

Once it was dark, Petit's group took a bow and arrow from one of their bags and fired 250 feet of steel cable from one tower to the other. *Fizzzzzzzzzzzzzzz!*

Then they settled in to rest.

A little past seven in the morning, when the streets below them were starting to stir, Philippe grasped his balancing pole and stepped out onto the wire. He had nearly reached the other side, when he saw the police had raced up the far tower and were waiting to arrest him. So he turned around, returned to the middle of the wire and—get this—he danced. He stood all the way up there and he danced. The police were shouting at him to walk to safety; the crowds down below were pointing at the speck high above them, and there he was laughing and dancing, as full of life as anyone could ever want to be.

When the police did finally get their hands on him, they let him go. People loved what he'd done so much, his only punishment, if you can call it that, was to perform his high-wire act for children in Central Park. The towers' owners even gave him a lifetime pass to the observation deck at the top of the towers and asked him to sign one of the buildings' steel beams.

So you see where I got the idea.

Now, as you know, I'm no tightrope artist. But I do love a thrill. Remember when I ski-jumped backwards off the roof of the cinema in Lake Placid?

After reading about Philippe Petit, I couldn't get his achievement out of my head. That very night, I went straight from work to Gramercy Park and slung a rope between two low trees and started teaching myself to walk along it. I can't tell you how many times I fell off, sometimes landing on my feet, other times hard on my hands or knees. But I kept at it. After dozens of tries, I managed two steps, then three, four, and five. I learned to keep breathing and focus on a still object ahead of me to keep my balance. I got some pretty strange looks from people walking their dogs, but you know New Yorkers, Charlie: they don't get involved in other people's business, especially when they look half-crazy.

As I gained confidence, I moved my practice to Central Park, to two American oak trees near the Great Lawn, where I could tie the rope a little higher and tighter, eight feet or so off the ground, about one and a half times you. It hurt even more when I fell, and if I didn't manage to land on my feet, it really hurt. I had to make sure the ground below me was just grass, no sticks or rocks. I'd roll up my trousers to just below my knee, take off my jacket and tie, and practice from early evening till dark. Eventually, I found a good long stick to hold and keep me balanced. I began waking early and racing up to the park at dawn to get in a couple of hours of rope walking before work. In my office, I laid a string along the floor and would pace along it, one bare foot in front of the other, while reading manuscripts. George, that discouraging goon, would walk by my door and shake his head.

After three months of this routine, I felt ready. I had learned to keep moving forward, not to wait for the rope to stop wobbling beneath me. I could stop, turn around, and keep walking. I could even walk backward, feeling my way along with my feet. But most important, I'd learned not to look down.

So two weeks ago, I went to a hardware store in Long Island City to buy what I needed: 100 feet of steel cable. Hooks to hold it tight. And at an outdoor store, I found a crossbow which I could use to fire the cable across the chasm of Fifth Avenue.

I checked the weather forecast to ensure a clear day, without much wind. And then I waited. Have you ever looked forward to something so much, Charlie, that you couldn't go to sleep? Or when you wake up in the morning, realize you can't even remember you went to sleep because you must have just drifted off from the exhaustion of anticipation? I stood at the window of my apartment on Lexington Avenue just willing the sun up from its bed. I saw its rosy fingers creeping up and wanted to reach out and yank them up high into the sky.

I met George for breakfast at a diner on 21st Street, around the corner from the office. I didn't have the stomach to eat, but watched George consume his usual Hungry Man special, mountains of eggs, pancakes, and bacon. As he slurped away, we went over the details. At noon, he was to walk over to the building across the street and nonchalantly make his way to the roof. Nonchalance does not come naturally to George (nor does élan, panache, sangfroid, or any of those other French-sounding

221

qualities). But we were going to try. Once up on the roof he was to wait for me to shoot over the cable and then bolt it tight. Watching George dribble ketchup onto the lapel of his jacket, I did wonder if I'd chosen the right companion for this adventure.

The morning inched by. I tried to concentrate on my work, but couldn't help looking out of my window every few moments to check on the weather, the speed of the clouds as they scudded across the sky.

Shortly before noon, I noticed George scuttle past my office door. I watched him walk across the street. I gathered the duffel bag which contained the cable and crossbow and sidled out towards the elevator.

"Whistler! In my office. Now!"

It was my boss, Mr. Crabtree.

I turned and walked back towards him.

"Where are you off to?"

"To drop something off. Some manuscripts," I said, pointing at the bag. He beckoned me into his office.

"I'm concerned," he began, once we'd both sat down. "About your failure to attract authors. What do you have to say about it?" He was staring at my bag, as it clanked when I set it down.

About my professional failings, he was absolutely right. I've always loved books and reading, but never been one for cocktail parties and readings and all the other palaver which passes for business in the publishing world. And since catching this rope-walking bug, I'd had no time for anything but work and lurking around parks trying to find my balance. No wonder I hadn't brought in any new authors. I hadn't met any.

"I will try harder."

Crabtree stared at me through his lizardy eyes.

222

"That's it?"

I was desperate to get out of there. I was thinking of George standing on the roof opposite, wondering where I'd got to. My bag felt like an unexploded bomb beside me.

"I'll make sure to get out more."

"You certainly will, Whistler. Your future at this company depends on it."

He waved me away, shaking his head. What an imbecile, he must have thought. But I didn't care. I was gone. Through his door, down the corridor, and out, up the fire exit stairs, pounding up flight after flight. When I finally burst through the door at the top, I could see George on the roof of the building opposite, turning to go back down.

"Wait!" I shouted. He turned and tapped his watch in frustration. I walked to the edge of the roof and looked down. Bad idea. I closed my eyes and stepped back.

I took out the crossbow and cable, threaded the cable onto a bolt, rested the bow against my shoulder, and fired. The bolt soared over Fifth Avenue and thudded into the roof opposite. George picked it up and clipped it onto a metal stand, which he then wedged under the ledge running round the roof. I pulled it tight on my side and clipped it fast. I yanked off my shoes and socks and tucked them into the duffel bag. I removed my tie so it didn't flap in my face. Then I picked up the balancing stick I had been using in the park, which I'd stashed up on the roof a few days earlier, and without a moment's pause stepped up onto the ledge and out onto the wire.

As I took that first step, it felt as though my stomach had dropped straight down, between my legs all the way to the street below. I fixed my eyes on the water tower on the roof opposite me and began to walk

223

forward. "It's no different from the park," I kept telling myself. "Just a bit higher." A pigeon landed a few feet in front of me. George began yelling at it. It didn't move. I kept walking. A third of the way over, I began to relax. My breathing began to even out. By the time I got to the middle, I felt giddy. I turned and bounced a little. I could hear voices from the offices in the buildings all around me, people shouting out encouragement. I wiggled my hips a little, in tribute to Petit's dance. Then I kept going.

A sharp gust of wind struck me flush on the left side and I wobbled dangerously. But I regained control and kept going.

"Come on," yelled George, waving me over.

But I wasn't ready to come on. I stopped and looked around. There I was, 200 feet up over Manhattan, surrounded by clean air and wheeling pigeons.

Now this was living.

Behind me I saw Crabtree and two policemen standing on the roof of my office building, pointing and yelling. But the wind carried away their words. For that moment, I was untouchable.

I kept walking towards George.

When I reached him, he grabbed my balancing stick and pulled me in. He hugged me and slapped me on the back.

"You did it! You did it!" I'd never seen him so excited.

I was still barefoot when we returned to the office. As I walked through the door, I could sense people were avoiding looking at me. This was no hero's welcome. No one even said hello. Standing by my office door were Crabtree and the police officers.

"Ya' need to come with us," said one of the officers, handing me my shoes.

"And when you're gone, don't bother coming back," said Crabtree.

I didn't argue. I wanted to say the disturbance was entirely private, for my benefit only. But I remember Dad always telling us, policemen don't like it when people get clever with them. I simply laced up my shoes and went along to the station, where I was issued with a $50 fine and let go.

As I walked home, up through Manhattan at rush hour, through the throngs pushing towards Grand Central Terminal, I felt this sense of lightness, as if I were floating above this magnificent island, gazing down. Part of me felt stupid for losing my job, but only a small part of me. I am still young and capable and bold, I thought, and have no need to spend my life living up to the demands of the Crabtrees of this world. That night, I sat alone in my apartment, ate a carton of Chinese fried rice and drank a soda, and felt freer than I had ever since I came to New York.

I slept deeply that night, more deeply than I had since I'd been gripped by my deranged ambition. And when I woke it was 9:00 a.m. already, and my telephone was ringing. I ignored it. As I staggered to the bathroom to brush my teeth, it rang again, and again as I turned on the stove to make coffee. Either someone was dead or I owed them money. Finally I picked it up. It was George.

"Where are you?" he said.

"Where do you think I am, you clod? In my apartment, where you called me."

"Well, you need to get to your office."

"Crabtree fired me. Don't you recall?"

"Get over here now." I could hear Crabtree in the background yelling, "Is he there?"

I took my time. Sipped my coffee. Dressed carefully. Had a long hot shower. Then stepped out into the warm morning. I must tell you, Charlie, everything seemed warmer that morning. The blue of the sky. The yellow of the taxicabs. The green of the doormen's coats outside the fancy apartment buildings. I noticed the arrangement of the flowers in the beds running down Park Avenue. The strange little dogs people have. And finally I came to my office. As I pushed open the door to the building, the man behind reception rose and greeted me, the first time in three years.

"Lovely day, Mr. Whistler," he said.

I took the elevator up to the 12th floor. When the doors opened, I saw the corridor leading to my office was packed with people.

"There he is!" shouted a man I'd never met. I was pulled out of the elevator and jostled along to my office. George materialized beside me.

"They've been arriving ever since the office opened."

I got to my office, pushed open the door, and fell inside. Crabtree was standing looking sullen.

"It appears your adventure has captured the imagination of every writer of adventure and derring-do in the country," he said. "They all want to work with the tightrope-walking editor."

Much as I disliked Crabtree, I didn't want to humiliate him.

"Well," I said, secretly thanking my good luck. "Send 'em in."

Your brother,
Frank

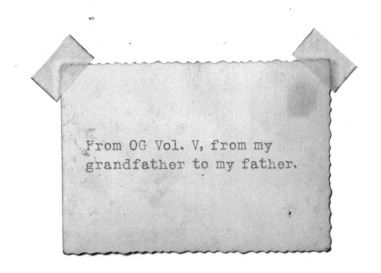

From OG Vol. V, from my
grandfather to my father.

January 28, 1986

My dear Charlie,

Have you ever wondered what makes a person take risks? Why some
never leave their homes and their offices and their old routines and
others lace up their boots to stride forth? Today, the space shuttle
Challenger exploded 73 seconds after taking off from Cape Canaveral
in Florida. Seven astronauts died: Michael Smith, Dick Scobee, Judith
Resnik, Ronald McNair, Ellison Onizuka, Gregory Jarvis, and Christa
McAuliffe. President Reagan came on television and said they "had that
special grace, that special spirit that says 'Give me a challenge and I'll
meet it with joy.'" He said their deaths might be hard for children to
understand, but that this is what happens when men and women take

risks and dare to expand our horizons. He ended his speech by quoting from a poem called "High Flight" by John Gillespie Magee Jr., who died while serving in the Royal Canadian Air Force in World War Two. Magee was 19. "High Flight" is about the thrill of flying, but it's also about daring the untried, the impossible, about taking a challenge and meeting it with joy. Reagan only used a line or two. You should have the whole thing. There are days a father appreciates his children more than others and today, when we lost seven bold adventurers, is one of them.

Oh! I have slipped the surly bonds of earth
And danced the skies on laughter-silvered wings;
Sunward I've climbed, and joined the tumbling mirth
Of sun-split clouds—and done a hundred things
You have not dreamed of—wheeled and soared and swung
High in the sunlit silence. Hov'ring there,
I've chased the shouting wind along, and flung
My eager craft through footless halls of air.

Up, up the long, delirious, burning blue
I've topped the wind-swept heights with easy grace.
Where never lark, or even eagle flew—
And, while with silent, lifting mind I've trod
The high untrespassed sanctity of space,
Put out my hand and touched the face of God.

Left to right: *Christa McAuliffe, Gregory Jarvis, Judith Resnik, Dick Scobee, Ronald McNair, Michael Smith, Ellison Onizuka.*

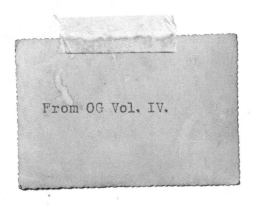

September 21st, 1975
Los Gatos, California

Charlie,

Here in Northern California for the week and I dropped by Andy Capp's Tavern in Sunnyvale where I picked up a strange magazine called the *Whole Earth Catalog*. It was published for four years from 1968 to 1972 but is still passed around like it's a holy text. "We are as gods and might as well get good at it," it claimed. "So far, remotely done power and glory—as via government, big business, formal education, church—has succeeded to the point where gross defects obscure actual gains. In response to this dilemma and to these gains a realm of intimate, personal power is developing—power of the individual to conduct his own education, find his own inspiration, shape his own environment, and share his adventure with whoever is interested. Tools that aid this process are sought and promoted by the WHOLE EARTH CATALOG." Lots of seeds and shovels and generators, as far as I can tell.

But then in the back, they redeem their craziness with this one page showing light glinting off the earth and these words: Stay Hungry. Stay Foolish.

Not a bad code for living. There's a Whistler spirit to this part of Northern California. They don't settle for the way things are. They want to keep learning and changing. I think I might stick around and look for opportunities.

Love,
Frank

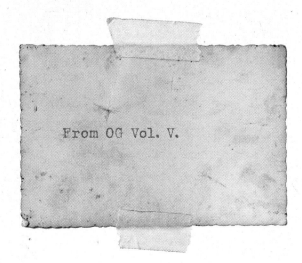

Yorkshire, England, 1982

Dear Charlie,

Driving from Manchester to Scunthorpe, I stopped for lunch in the town of Sherburn-in-Elmet. A crowd had gathered in the main square to watch a leathery old man wearing a flat cap, tweed jacket, and baggy white pants. Around his ankles, his pants were tied up with string. Another man stood beside him holding aloft two snarling ferrets. I asked one of the men in the crowd what was going on.

"Ferret-legging," he said. "This fellow thinks he can beat the record." Still mystified, I listened to the announcer.

"Ladies and gentlemen. The rules are as follows. Two ferrets, sharp in tooth and claw, will be deposited down the challenger's trousers. An inspection has been conducted to ascertain that the challenger is wearing no underwear of any kind. There is also room inside his trousers for the ferrets to travel from leg to leg. Once the ferrets have been deposited, the challenger's belt will be tied so there is no chance of the ferrets escaping. The clock will start the moment the belt is fastened. The current record stands at six hours and thirty-two minutes. Mr. Midgeley, are you ready?"

The crowd clapped. Midgeley nodded and held open his pants. The announcer dropped in the two ferrets. Midgeley buckled his belt and then looked to the heavens. The church clock rang noon. The crowd cheered as the ferrets surged up and down Midgeley's legs. But he kept staring up without so much as a grimace.

As it started to drizzle, the crowd thinned out. I went into a nearby

pub for lunch. When I emerged an hour later, Midgeley was still there, staring upwards, the rain falling into his face, his clothes drenched. The announcer was sitting in a makeshift booth to the left of the stage reading the newspaper and eating a meat pie.

"Is he really going to stand there for six hours?" I asked.

"Longer if he can."

"Why the white pants?"

"Trousers, you mean? So we can see the blood when the ferrets bite."

"They don't seem to have bitten him at all," I said, pointing to the pristine pants.

"Ay," said the announcer, beckoning me in. "Seeing as you're clearly not from 'ere, I'll tell you Midgeley's secret. Most ferret-leggers think it's all about enduring pain, that if you can just take enough bites from the little blighters and put up with it, you'll win. Not Midgeley. He's cleverer than that. A retired headmaster, you see. And an animal lover. He jiggles his legs around and rubs them together, so the ferrets feel cozy instead of imprisoned. Instead of biting him, they just curl up in a ball next to his shoes." I looked and saw a bulge around his ankles.

"But what happens when they wake up?"

"You're asking the right questions, lad." And with that he went back to reading his newspaper.

I had to leave, but the next day, I was eager to find out if Midgeley had triumphed. There he was on the front page of the *Yorkshire Evening Post* looking forlorn. He'd fallen five minutes short because his legs had started to cramp and he couldn't stay standing. Still, my admiration for him remains unbounded.

Two days later, I stopped in Egremont up in the Lake District on the day of the town's Crab Fair, which has been held every year since 1267.

(The Crab refers to the crab apples handed out to the children by the Lord of the Manor of Egremont.) The highlight of the fair is the World Gurning Championships. To "gurn" is to make a funny face. Contestants have to put their head through a horse collar and then make the silliest face they can. The real crowd-pleasers are the toothless elderly, who can often lift their lower lips right over their noses. If Midgley ever chose to enter, I'll bet he's saved up enough funny faces to close it down forever.

With love,
Dad

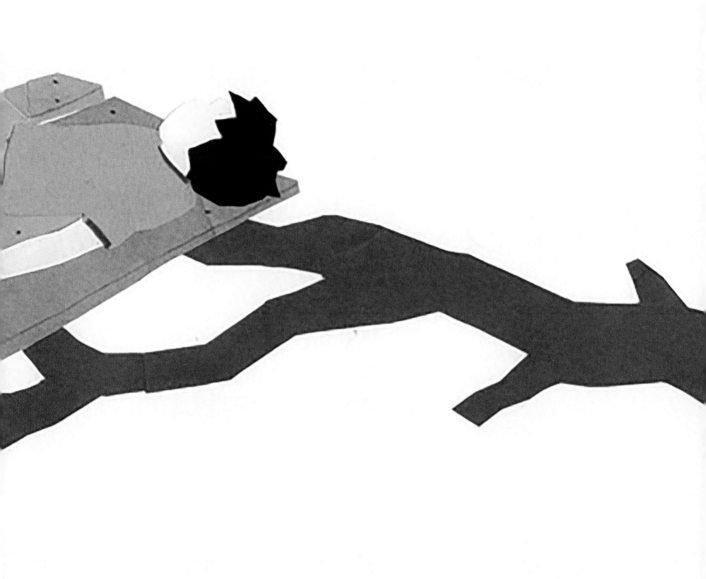

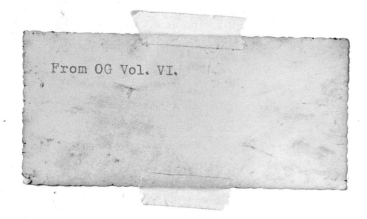

August 2015

I was thinking of building a tree house by the lake, so my Dad and I went to the library to do some research. But the plans in all the books were far too complicated. It seemed like you had to be a combination master architect and carpenter to build one of these things, with roofs and staircases and balconies. Dad called his friend Spencer, who builds climbing frames for children. These aren't just any old climbing frames. They are fantasy climbing frames, swirling upwards in crazy shapes. I asked him: what kind of tree house would you build?

Spencer said that when he was a kid, his dad built him this elaborate tree house. But he never much liked it. So he rarely used it. But what he did love to do was climb a particular tree with a view down to a lake and sit up there and daydream. So one day, he took a few pieces of wood and wedged them into the tree's split trunk. Each day, he took a few more pieces, until eventually he had a kind of structure up there. And he would go there to while away the time, enjoying the view and that feeling of floating high above the earth, free from every trouble.

When we were driving up to the Adirondacks earlier this summer, we stopped sixty miles north of New York City. On the eastern bank of the Hudson River is an old factory building which has been turned into a museum, called Dia: Beacon. In what used to be the loading docks are four giant metal sculptures. Each one weighs a couple of tons, but as you approach them, they seem as weightless as sheets of paper balanced on their sides. The moment you walk inside them, you feel disoriented and off balance, as if the very air around you has changed. Like being in a tree house.

They were created by an American artist, Richard Serra, whose father had been a pipe fitter in the San Francisco shipyards. When Richard grew up and became a sculptor, he decided to work with the kind of enormous sheets of steel he had seen in the shipyards, bending, curling, and tilting them to create fantastical spaces.

Now, over to Dad:

Thank you, Charlie. The idea for the *Torqued Ellipses* at Dia came to Serra on a visit to a tiny church in Rome, which sits squashed into the corner of a block. It's called San Carlo alle Quattro Fontane, St. Charles with the Four Fountains. It has four fountains built into its facade. The church was built in the 1600s by Francesco Borromini, a gloomy loner who took little pleasure in being one of the most famous architects of his day. His buildings are joyous, swerving and curving, swelling and billowing like the sails on a ship. Inside San Carlo alle Quattro Fontane, Borromini rejected the classic circular dome popular in other churches at the time, in favor of an ellipse. It suited the tight space. But if you stand inside the church and look up, you feel quite wobbly.

(gruesome postscript: Borromini eventually put an end to all his moping around by killing himself. But his suicide did not go quite

239

as planned. He ran a sword through his stomach, but survived long enough to describe the event in his diary, complete his will, and receive the last rites before dying.)

After seeing Borromini's church, Serra tried to recreate the dome's ellipse effect, to capture the same billowing and swerving feeling Borromini made out of stone. As you said, if you walk or run through his *Torqued Ellipses*, you feel the air closing in and opening up again around you, the light changing, even your sense of balance seeming to shift as the angle of the walls takes you by surprise.

241

Digging through the stacks of papers in the attic, I found this photograph taken in 1922 and published in *National Geographic*. It shows a boy standing in the Great Zimbabwe, a ruined city in southern Africa which was the capital of the Shona people between the 11th and 15th centuries. The word Zimbabwe means house of stone. Its wealth came from gold mining and trading. Archaeologists suspect it was eventually abandoned because it became overpopulated and the land around became arid as it was stripped of trees. The way he's standing there against the great, curving, granite wall reminded me of you inside the Serra.

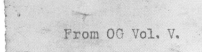

February 1979

Dear Charlie,

Here in Paris, people are still scratching their heads about the Pompidou Center. Things that are usually inside a building, pipes, elevators, are outside. One of its architects explained that he never liked using elevators and escalators deep inside buildings. So he put them on the outside. If he was going to be moving up and down, why not have a view? Suddenly, it all makes sense!

Love,
Dad

POMPIDOU - CENTRE

May 2006

Early May in New Mexico's high southwestern desert. We drove up to a wooden building on the main square of the small town of Quemado. A man in a cowboy hat came out, tossed our bags into the back of his pickup truck and told us to climb in the cabin. He drove us for 45 minutes down a long dirt track. The rest of the world disappeared from view. All we could see was empty land, shades of brown and green, sweeping up towards mountains. Suddenly, there was a log cabin, the kind you see in old western movies, gray and weather-beaten with a rail for horses along one side. Beyond it lay row after row of silver poles, flashing and disappearing in the sunlight, like fish in a stream. It was *The Lightning Field*.

Walter De Maria was born in 1935 in California. He has been a drummer, composer, and film producer as well as a sculptor. Starting in the 1970s, he began working on something he called Land Art. It was a way of making art out of the great landscapes of America, the astonishing terrain, light, and weather.

He wanted to make people think about their place on the earth and within the universe. That takes some imagination.

He bought this vast plot of land in New Mexico and installed 400 steel poles, each one 20 feet 7.5 inches, over a grid one mile by one kilometer. The cabin was left here so people can come and stay overnight. After supper, we sat out on the porch as the sun went down. Every minute, the light reflected differently from the poles. The sky was so vast, it felt like you were watching the weather as it happened. We watched the clouds creeping across the sky towards us. Slowly, as the light faded, the sky filled with stars, more than I had ever seen. It felt like the dark sky was just a moth-eaten curtain and behind it shone a brilliant light which pierced thousands of tiny holes. No one said much. We just felt the stillness of the air, every slight change in the light and temperature.

A rumble. A cloud appeared over the mountains in the distance. It was just after 10:00 p.m. We wrapped our blankets tightly around ourselves and waited. The first drops of rain splashed on our cold faces. A single flash of lightning cut through the darkness. It missed the rows of poles. We waited. The clouds and thunder rumbled closer. Another flash, another miss.

Then a strike! The lightning hit a pole in the far corner of the field and ricocheted from pole to pole. It was like watching a giant electrical circuit blow up in front of us. Then another strike, on a pole closer to the center. The whole plain lit up, as if it were a floodlit baseball park. Then the storm moved on.

We stayed where we were, huddled beneath the porch, staring out into the damp dark night, which hummed with electricity. Only the tips of the poles shone in the starlight. I had never felt so small in the face of the universe. Nor so excited to be part of it.

August 2014

MW

Darling Charlie,

A wise man once said that what doesn't get wept gets written. And I know what a dreadful summer you have had. Bullies seemed to lurk around every corner. And then of course poor Frenzy, run over so quickly and cruelly on the road around the lake. We shall get a new dog, I promise, another beagle, but I realize none can ever replace Frenzy. There is no friendship in the world quite like that between a boy and his first dog. You and Frenzy grew up together. He yanked you along on walks. You got in trouble together. Do you remember when he was a puppy and he rampaged through the living room, tearing apart cushions and chewing up the carpet? And you tried to take the blame? As if we would ever believe you were the one eating our cushions!

But think about this. Most people live far longer than animals, not counting tortoises! If you choose to love a pet, chances are you will see it die. All that matters is that while they are alive, you love them as best

Frenzy

Confucius

you can. You did that with Frenzy. And you will do it with many more pets over the course of your life, I'm sure of it. (Quick, which president kept a wallaby in the White House? *Calvin Coolidge.*)

The bigger challenge for you is simply to be happy and to find that happiness within yourself. People often say they are happy when they are wallowing in a warm bath or eating a bowl of ice cream. But really, being happy is an activity. Happiness involves doing, thinking, and feeling. It is about knowing who you are, what you do best, and what you enjoy. It is about being thoughtful and kind towards others and yet, deep down, knowing that the only opinion which really matters is your own.

If you're comfortable doing what you do, you're most likely happy. If you're uncomfortable or care too much what other people think, you are unhappy. "To thine own self be true," Polonius advised his son Laertes in *Hamlet*. Be true to yourself and you'll be true to others. Life is just much simpler that way.

I realize that when boys and girls your own age taunt or mock you, it can hurt. But the only reason that it hurts is because you care. When people are cruel to others, it is a sign of their own unhappiness. Bullies are to be pitied, not feared. They see you wandering along, lost in your thoughts, and they make fun of you, because they are jealous of your contentment. They believe they can only feel bigger by making you feel smaller.

You know that small picture in the hallway, at the bottom of the back stairs? I know it's covered in dust and you've probably run past it hundreds of times without stopping to look. It's of a serious-looking guy with long tufts of hair coming out of his chin, not really a beard, more like the leftovers of a beard. That's the Chinese philosopher, Confucius, or K'ung Fu Tze, who lived a roller coaster of a life two and a half thousand years ago. He spent most of it in a small town called Lu, where he was keeper of stores, superintendent of herds, and finally chief magistrate. He was a good judge, but his enemies forced him from office and he spent the next 14 years wandering around China with a group of followers studying and teaching. Only towards the end of his life did he return to Lu.

His experiences allowed him to think deeply about what makes a good life and a good person. The good person, he said, "does what is proper to the station in which he is; he does not desire to go beyond this. In a position of wealth and honor, he does what is proper to a position of wealth and honor. In a poor and low position, he does what is proper to a poor and low position. Situated among barbarous tribes, he does what is proper to a situation among barbarous tribes. In a position of sorrow and difficulty, he does what is proper to a position of sorrow and difficulty. He can find himself in no situation in which he is not himself. In a high situation, he does not treat with contempt his inferiors. In a low situation, he does not court the favor of his superiors. He rectifies himself, and seeks nothing from others, so that he has no dissatisfactions. He does not murmur against Heaven, nor grumble against men. Thus it is that the good man is quiet and calm, waiting for the appointments of Heaven, while the mean man walks in dangerous paths, looking for lucky occurrences."

This is you, Charlie. You are quiet and calm and caring. You do not grumble—without very good reason. You are respectful of whatever situation you find yourself in, funny with your friends, polite and interested with adults, kind towards the old.

Five hundred years after Confucius, the Roman Emperor Marcus Aurelius—another beard!—wrote at the end of a life filled with warfare and personal loss: "Very little is needed to make a happy life. It is all within yourself, in your way of thinking." Here was a man who could have everything, who ruled great swaths of the world. He could have eaten off gold plates and changed into new silk pajamas five times a day.

Marcus Aurelius

But when it came to being happy, he had no more nor less than the poorest man in his Empire: his heart, his mind, and his conscience.

When life turns choppy, some people panic, while others stay focused. Perhaps you've seen me reading books by Gabriel García Márquez. He's a Colombian author. People all over the world adore his books. But when he was a boy, he struggled at school. He hated homework and would put it off while he did what he really enjoyed, which was to play with his friends or read books. Of course, his problems only escalated. His schoolwork suffered. He was caught cheating. His teachers complained and his parents became cross. What could he do?

He wrote in his memoir that the answer was surprisingly simple. "If I paid attention in classes and did the assignments myself instead of copying them from my classmates, I would get a good grade and be able to read as much as I liked in my free hours, and lead my own life without exhausting all-night study sessions or useless fears."

Do what you must when you're meant to be doing it and life becomes a whole lot easier. There will always be bullies, as well as friends, trying to distract you and drag you off course, away from yourself and your sense of what is right for you. Don't let them, Charlie.

There's a phrase that kayakers use which I've always found useful. They say that the rock in the river is the

Gabriel García Márquez

river also. The obstacles in our path are part of the path. Don't ever feel cheated or hard done by if you have to overcome them.

The last thing I would say to you, Charlie, is to recall that we Whistlers are zestful people. The world and all of its remarkable contents fascinate us. From the humblest insect to the mightiest building, from the pattern on a dead tree branch to the arc of a rocket ship. In a world as interesting as ours there is no excuse for boredom, for turning over the same old problems and anxieties. You must look outward, engage, collect, gather, observe, and share. Anything is interesting if you make the effort to be interested.

There are few things worse when you're feeling down than to have someone blast away at you with a sermon-load of advice. I apologize if I've done that. But given how it pains all of us to see you so glum, I thought I should try.

Be restrained, Charlie, so you're not dependent on the opinions or wants of others. Be disciplined, so you can meet the needs of the world and still have time and energy for yourself. Be zestful, so the joys and mysteries of life do not pass you by.

Know that Frenzy had a wonderful life and that we shall soon get another beagle puppy to tear up our cushions and chew on our carpets. There is always another beagle.

And above all, Charlie, be yourself.

With all my love,
Mom

From OG Vol. II, July 1873, from the summer journal of Charles Wetherby Whistler.

Boatswain

I haven't much time for poets. Too much verse makes me queasy. And the next adult who thinks it'll be a fine idea to read a boy Longfellow—I'm shoving him in the lake. But then along comes this English rascal and poet Lord Byron and it's almost enough to change my mind. When he was a student, his university banned him from keeping a dog. So he kept a bear instead. He seemed to love animals more than he did people, whom he often treated badly. When his beloved dog Boatswain contracted rabies, Byron nursed him himself, regardless of the risk of contracting the fatal disease. And when Boatswain died, Byron, who was always in debt, paid for an elaborate stone monument to his dog. Cost be damned! I'll never care much for his flowery poems, but this is a dog lover's epitaph to admire:

> Near this spot are deposited the remains of one who possessed Beauty without Vanity, Strength without Insolence, Courage without Ferocity, and all the Virtues of Man without his Vices. This praise, which would be unmeaning Flattery, if inscribed over human ashes, is but a just Tribute to the Memory of BOATSWAIN, a Dog.

Now.

So this is us. Or a little piece of us. Or maybe it's just me. My selection from all these Whistler summers. I could have chosen a hundred other items for my Omnium Gatherum and you'd think me a different person altogether. And maybe I will. But I've made a start. And now it's your turn.

Find an empty book and start to fill it.

Tell me who you are.

Your friend always,
Charlie

Grandpa's hound Wagstaff.

ACKNOWLEDGMENTS

With thanks to Amber McMillan, Nancy Loeber, and Sarah Nicholls of the great Center for Book Arts in New York, for their contributions and enthusiasm. To Tina Bennett for her unflagging support and inspiration, and to Svetlana Katz for staying with Charlie Whistler all these years. To Jamie Byng for his exuberant backing, and to Cal Morgan, Laura Brown, and Leah Carlson-Stanisic at HarperCollins, and Jenny Lord at Canongate, for bringing Charlie to life. To the Resurrection Episcopal Day School in New York and to the Washington Montessori and Litchfield Intermediate Schools in Litchfield County. To Trattie Davies, May Bogdanovics, and Visko Hatfield for crucial support at crucial moments. To Luke and Tic Bridgeman. To Sandy Neubauer for introducing me to Bob Parker, a member of the Whistler family made flesh and blood. To James Lyle and Todd Snyder for much-needed fishing escapades both Whistler-ish and not so much. To my godchildren, Eveleen, Valentine, Rose, Camilla, and Reg. To Cindy, to Victoria, to Marcia and Simon. To Margret, for all your love, humor, elegance, and sanity. And to my splendid boys, Augie and Hugo. Like it or not, fellas, this one's for you.

PERMISSIONS

Canoeists by Sarah Nicholls.

Boy on Lake by Philip Delves Broughton.

Two in a Fishing Boat by Robert Parker.

Whistler Compound, Library of Congress, Prints & Photographs Division, Detroit Publishing Company Collection, LC-D4-36943.

Man Carrying Canoe, Library of Congress, Prints & Photographs Division, Detroit Publishing Company Collection, LC-D4-36933.

Canoes Beside Dock, Library of Congress, Prints & Photographs Division, Detroit Publishing Company Collection, LC-D4-14873.

Loon by Sarah Nicholls.

Orson Phelps, New York State Archives, Conservation Dept. Photographic prints and negatives, 14297-87, Box 261, no. 57-L-278-MIS.

Meditating Monk, Library of Congress, Prints & Photographs Division. LC-DIG-jpd-00308.

Adirondacks Map by Verplanck Colvin.

Canoe on a Lake, Library of Congress, Prints & Photographs Division, Detroit Publishing Company Collection, LC-D4-36927.

Man with Canoe by Robert Parker.

Mice, Mice, Snakes by Robert Parker.

Snakes and Mice by Robert Parker.

Casting Number Two by Winslow Homer, 1836–1910. 1894, watercolor over graphite on wove paper. sheet: 38.5 × 54.5 cm (15 3/16 × 21 7/16 in.). Courtesy of the National Gallery of Art. Gift of Ruth K. Henschel in memory of her husband, Charles R. Henschel 1975.92.2.

Flag Pole on Lawn by Robert Parker.

Dragoons by Robert Parker.

Drunken Dragoon by Robert Parker.

Bombs Bursting in Air by Robert Parker.

Logrolling Lumberjacks by Robert Parker.

Flag Folding by Nancy Loeber.

Hungry Hoard at Nathan's by Al Almuller. New York World-Telegram and the Sun Newspaper Photograph Collection. Library of Congress. LC-DIG-ds-05428.

Home of the International Hot Dog Eating Contest by @wOOkie, courtesy of Creative Commons.

Teddy Roosevelt rowing by Robert Parker.

TR's Night Ride by Robert Parker.

Raquette Lake Railway Ticket public domain.

Adirondack Company's Railroad Ticket, courtesy of the Adirondack Museum.

Pony Express Map by William Henry Jackson, 1951. Library of Congress, Geography and Map Division.

Mail Flight by Robert Parker.

Statue of Theodore Roosevelt Outside the American Museum of Natural History and Close-up of His Head with Spikes by Lucinda Frame. © Lucinda Frame.

Soldier by Robert Parker.

Farmer on the Back of a Truck. Farmer on a Load of Hay, Farmers' Market, Weatherford, Texas, by Russell Lee. May 1939. U.S. Farm Security Administration/Office of War Information. Library of Congress, Prints and Photographs Division. LC-DIG-fsa-8a26549.

Voyage a la Lune, Library of Congress. LC-DIG-ppmsca-02337.

1964 World's Fair Photo by Carol Highsmith. Carol M. Highsmith Archive. Library of Congress. LC-DIG-highsm-12902.

Let's Go to the Fair, courtesy of General Motors LLC.

John Muir, Library of Congress Prints and Photographs Division, LC-USZ62-55012.

John Muir's Notebook. Muir Hails a Palmetto. John Muir Papers, Holt-Atherton Special Collections, University of the Pacific Library. © 1984 Muir-Hanna Trust.

John Muir Up a Tree by Robert Parker.

Eratosthenes and the Circumference of the Earth by Nancy Loeber.

Adirondack Carry. Library of Congress, Prints & Photographs Division, Detroit Publishing Company Collection, LC-D4-71230.

Happy Barber, National Geographic, 1929. Basil Avezathe, estate unknown.

Suez Canal by Robert Parker.

Through the Khyber Pass, courtesy of the Library of Congress. LC-LOT 10526 (J) #120.

Afghan Mosque by Robert Parker.

Buzkashi Horseman by Sarah Nicholls.

Boys in Helmets. January 1932, *Modern Mechanics & Inventions*, published by Fawcett Publications bought by CBS in 1977.

Beebe's Bathysphere by Sarah Nicholls.

James Cameron's Sub. © Mark Thiessen/National Geographic Creative.

1934 Winter Olympics Poster: Up Where Winter Calls to Play. By Jack Rivolta, Works Projects Administration Poster Collection. Library of Congress. LC-USZC4-4510.

Bobsledders, courtesy of the Adirondack Museum.

Skiing off the Cinema by Robert Parker.

Spot the Frogman, courtesy of the Adirondack Museum.

Map of Wallface Rescue by Nancy Loeber.

Campfire in Woods by Robert Parker.

Moon During the Day by Nancy Loeber.

ADK 46er Badge, courtesy of the Adirondack 46ers.

Banana Shake by Sarah Nicholls.

How to Throw a Football, Boy Surrounded by Older Players, courtesy Library of Congress, Prints & Photographs Division, photograph by Harris & Ewing, LC-DIG-hec-39802.

How to Throw a Baseball by Nancy Loeber.

Moonshot! by Nancy Loeber.

Base Stealer by Nancy Loeber.

Roald Amundsen, courtesy of NOAA/Department of Commerce.

Robert Scott on Skis, licensed with permission of the Scott Polar Research Institute, University of Cambridge.

Scott's Dog Chris Listening to the Gramophone, licensed with permission of the Scott Polar Research Institute, University of Cambridge.

El Lagarto, the Leaping Lizard by Robert Parker.

Long House by Sarah Nicholls.

Funny Face Mask by Sarah Nicholls.

Bear Roaring by Sarah Nicholls.

Iroquois Indians, courtesy of Library of Congress Prints and Photographs Division. LC-USZ62-127674.

Great Horned Owl by John James Audubon, courtesy of the Audubon Society.

ABOUT THE AUTHOR

Philip Delves Broughton has been a journalist, a foreign correspondent, and a columnist reporting from all over the world. He is the author of the nonfiction bestsellers *Ahead of the Curve: Two Years at Harvard Business School* and *The Art of the Sale: Learning from the Masters About the Business of Life*. He grew up in England and received his BA and MA in Classics from New College, Oxford, and an MBA from Harvard Business School. He lives in Connecticut with his wife, two sons, and two dogs.

HarperCollins books may be purchased for educational, business, or sales promotional use. For information, please e-mail the Special Markets Department at SPsales@harpercollins.com.

FIRST EDITION

DESIGNED BY LEAH CARLSON-STANISIC

Tape and notecard graphics throughout by Picsfive/Shutterstock, Inc.
Photo corner images throughout by LiliGraphi/Shutterstock, Inc.
Paper background by Paladin12/Shutterstock, Inc.

Library of Congress Cataloging-in-Publication Data has been applied for.

ISBN: 978-0-06-232361-3

16 17 18 19 20   OV/RRD   10 9 8 7 6 5 4 3 2 1